Wayne Curtis

GOOSE LANE

Published by Goose Lane Editions with the assistance of the Canada Council
and the New Brunswick Department of Municipalities, Culture and Housing,
1996. First published in 1994 by New Ireland Press.

Some of the chapters in this book have been previously published in *The
Atlantic Salmon Journal, The Atlantic Advocate, Atlantic Insight, Outdoor
Atlantic, Eastern Woods and Waters, The Maritime Sportsman, Wilderness
Trails, The Moncton Times-Transcript, The Daily Gleaner, The Miramichi
Leader, Miramichi Weekend, New Maritimes,* and in the books *Currents in the
Stream* (Goose Lane Editions, 1988) and *One Indian Summer* (Goose Lane
Editions, 1994).

Cover design by Robinson + Greenwood Graphic Design Ltd.
Cover photo courtesy of Tom Pero, *Wild Steelhead & Atlantic Salmon.*
Fly illustrations by George Thompson from Taff Price's, *Fly Patterns: An
International Guide,* Western Producer Prairie Books.
Typeset by Cummings Imagesetting.
Printed in Canada by Gagné Printing.
  10 9 8 7 6 5 4 3 2

Canadian Cataloguing in Publication Data

Curtis, Wayne, 1945-
  Fishing the Miramichi
    ISBN 0-86492-181-0

1. Fishing — New Brunswick — Miramichi River — Guidebooks.
I. Title.

SH572.N4C87 1996   799.1'1'0971521   C96-950026-2

Goose Lane Editions
469 King Street
Fredericton, NB
CANADA E3B 1E5

To my three sons and fishing pals:
Jeff, Jason and Steven

Contents

Foreword

Wayne Curtis grew up near Blackville, New Brunswick, on a farm which bordered on the Miramichi River. His father being an outfitter and guide, the river, with all its quirks and idiosyncracies, became as familiar to him as his own name. He has spent most of his life honing his skills as a knowledgeable fisherman and conscientious river-person. Indeed, the river is now and always has been his first love.

Fly-fishing has always been of great interest to me, and two years ago I had the good fortune to fish with Mr. Curtis. This began what was to prove to be a far more detailed and unpredictable sport than I ever could have imagined. I found myself listening to instructions which sounded simple enough, yet somehow proved to be quite a challenge. "Timing," I was to hear over and over again, "it's all in the timing." The thrill of seeing that first sweet cast cover a small stretch of water brought with it an amazing sense of control. Then, just as I was beginning to feel like a graceful ballet dancer, I found myself tangled in line once again.

One cold May morning last spring, after a winter of dreaming about catching my first fish, we went black salmon fishing. We stood on the shore and casted out. I realized that my arm had forgotten some of its lessons, and I began to express my frustration rather emphatically. Shortly thereafter, Wayne invited me to try his rod and, lines still in the water, we switched over and I took his rod. Within seconds, I felt a pull and knew I had a fish on. Although we set it free, the exhilaration of those minutes as I beached the fish under the careful coaching of my guide was something I'll not likely forget. However, I should add that we have never talked about exactly when that fish actually took the fly.

Since then, I have hooked a grilse and was able to keep it on for several minutes before I eventually lost it. In all my excitement over catching my first fish, it had never occured to me that I might actually lose it!

These were the beginnings of my growing pains as a fly-fisher. I learned many things about fishing that summer, but none that stayed with me as well as the tremendous sense of respect for the river's welfare that Mr. Curtis instilled in me. He has a deep, nurturing attitude toward the river and its surroundings and a belief that we each have a responsibility to preserve its natural state.

As well as being a meticulous river-person and a fine writer, Mr. Curtis is also a master storyteller. His many experiences have afforded him a pool of anecdotes to draw from, some born of true detail and some purely fiction. But it isn't enough to simply have the stories. It is in the telling of them that he brings you back to that particular time and lets you experience the events for yourself.

It is the combination of this gift for storytelling with a wealth of solid information on the art of fly-fishing that makes this book a delightful read for even the most sedentary armchair angler. And for those of you who read Wayne Curtis and find yourselves irresistibly attracted by the thought of a well-timed, long cast of fly line across sparkling waters on a warm summer's day . . . see you on the river!

Maggie Martin

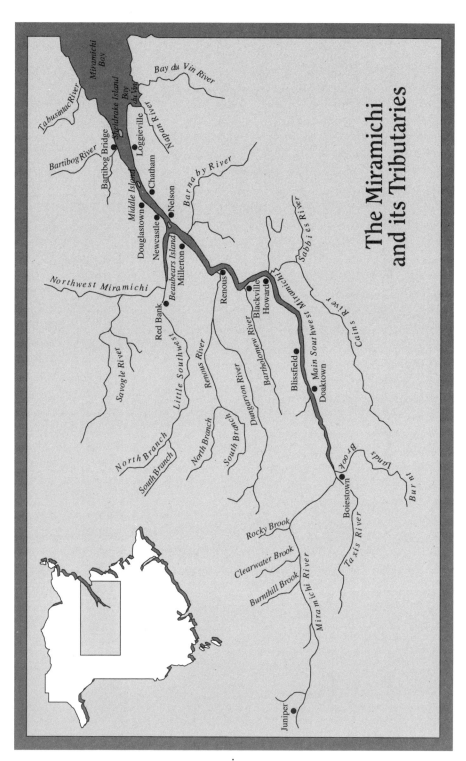

The Miramichi and its Tributaries

ONE
The Miramichi: A Yielding River

Durham Ranger

*M*iramichi is a Montagnais Indian word meaning "Micmac Land." The name is very apt, as the Micmac Indians had inhabited the Miramichi region for about ten thousand years before Jacques Cartier sailed across the river's mouth in 1534. The Micmacs themselves were said to have called the river Lustagoocheehk, which means "Little Godly River." The Micmacs have had a food fishery on the river for countless centuries and still do today, in spite of their constant struggle to retain this age-old right in the face of pressure from other user groups to give it up.

The headwaters of the main Southwest Miramichi River trickle from the hills above the tiny village of Juniper and flow northeast through the province of New Brunswick for some 220 miles before emptying into the Gulf of Saint Lawrence. From the air the river resembles a giant reptile with trailing legs, twisting and turning through a carpet of greenery, its great open mouth pointing northeast to catch the migrating south-bound salmon.

The Miramichi River is probably the best producer of Atlantic salmon today. It is certainly among North America's best, including such rivers as the Ungava, the Whale and the Eagle of northern Quebec, the Four Toe of

The Miramichi: A Yielding River

Labrador, the great Humber and Portland Creek of Newfoundland and so many fine rivers in Canada's Maritime provinces, the state of Maine and beyond. In fact, because of water temperatures and the growth rate of its parr the Miramichi produces more salmon annually than all rivers of Quebec combined. The Miramichi also offers excellent trout and shad fishing as well as a bass fishery in the estuary waters. But it is for its abundance of Atlantic salmon, its popularity as a recreational fishing paradise and its contribution to the provincial economy that this storied river has earned its fame.

The province, and indeed the country, is fortunate to have a river of this calibre, for a good river is the lifeblood of the land. Many rivers achieve a renown equal to the lands they inhabit. The Miramichi is no exception; in fact, it is probably better known internationally than the province it courses through. When we think of Brazil, we think of the Amazon; Egypt, the Nile; Germany, the Rhine, and so on. We may not know the names of the towns and villages along their banks, but we know of the rivers themselves. People on the other side of the world may not have heard of places like Newcastle or Fredericton, or even New Brunswick, but there is a good chance that they have heard of the Miramichi.

What makes a river great is much more than just the species that inhabit its waters. Its purity, its reproductive ability, its spirits and moods, its surrounding landscape and of course its people all contribute to a river's reputation. But the true source of the Miramichi's fame lies in its abundance of Atlantic salmon. The Atlantic salmon, the king of all fish, reproduces in greater numbers in this water system than any other in the world. Thus, the Miramichi is considered the mother of all salmon rivers. Even though it was not a good year, figures show that in 1993, 22,759 grilse were harvested during the bright salmon season in the Miramichi system, with another 5,861 grilse released, along with some 8,000 large salmon. This does not include the black salmon fishery.

The branches that make up the system are included in the overall statistics when the Miramichi rod and reel catch is calculated. These tributaries comprise Rocky Brook, McKeil Brook, Burnthill Brook, the Taxis River, Burnt Land Brook, Big Hole

Brook, the Cains River (with its tributary, the Sabbies River), the Bartholomew River, the Renous (with its tributary, the Dungarvon), the Barnaby River, the Northwest Miramichi (with its tributaries, the Little Southwest and the Big and Little Sevogle) the Black, the Napan and the Bartibog rivers. Many lesser streams help make up the system; too many to mention. The Napan, Tabusintac and the Bay du Vin rivers flow into Miramichi Bay and so are not considered tributaries of the Miramichi proper.

Due to its size, the main Southwest Miramichi produces more salmon consistently throughout the angling season than any of its tributaries. The tributaries, however, are not to be denied their finer moments. For periods while their runs are on, the tributaries can offer finer fishing than most other rivers in the province, each having its own runs of adult salmon, followed by a run of grilse. These rivers produce at different times, ranging from May on the Northwest Branch to October on the Cains and Bartibog.

Leaving the main river to fish the tributaries as they reach their peak runs can be rewarding. I once guided a man on an October holiday who landed six salmon in four days on the Cains River. Another year I took two Atlantic salmon on the Dungarvon River while on a canoeing weekend during the month of June. The key is to be on the right river at the right time.

The Northwest Miramichi and the Renous, along with their tributaries, are considered early-run salmon rivers. Statistics show that the Northwest Miramichi system produces the most fish in June and early July, with bright salmon entering the river as early as mid-May. While the Dungarvon is an early stream, the Renous, above its confluence, is a late June and July river which also produces a respectable fall run. The main Southwest Miramichi is early in small runs destined for tributaries, such as the Rocky Brook run. However, its major runs are in July and August (depending on water conditions), with the fall run (destined for the Cains and beyond) migrating the river in late September through October. The Cains, historically a late-run salmon river, has become a Mecca for anglers from September until the 15th of October. Although the Bartibog is barren of salmon until late October, it has a respectable trout fishery throughout the summer. A current copy of the Sport Fishing Summary offers information on river opening and closing days (these vary, depending on stocks and water conditions).

Unlike the main Southwest Miramichi, which offers only a small number of public-water pools, the tributaries have long stretches of open water that are accessible by road. Logging roads reach into the upper stretches of the Northwest Miramichi, Little Southwest and Sevogle. These are narrow, fast-flowing rivers with many good holding pools. There is plenty of public water available on the Little Southwest and to a lesser extent on the Northwest. The Sevogle also supplies many fine salmon pools which are public. However, the extreme upper reaches of these rivers are Crown Reserve waters and are banned to the general public (Crown Reserve stretches are acquired through a lottery: water stretches and available dates can be applied for through the Department of Natural Resources).

Many of these tributaries are a nice size for canoeing in the early summer, and the large salmon are usually hooked at this time. The Renous and its tributary, the Dungarvon, are also easy to reach. The Dungarvon, which is spring-fed, is probably the most consistent smaller salmon river in the province.

The Bartholomew River, the smallest tributary of the Miramichi freshwater system, was closed to all angling after the destruction of the old mill dam at Blackville, near the river's mouth, in 1977. For years it was kept as a hatchery stream. This came about as a result of pressure applied to government by the Miramichi Salmon Association and other interest groups to remove the dam and out-of-date fish ladder that existed there. This river is now open for angling on a trial basis.

The Cains River, the longest tributary of the Miramichi, is the nearest in character to the mother stream. While it has a reputation for its late runs, Dr. Richard Saunders, biologist at the Salmon Research Centre in St. Andrews, claims there is a respectable salmon run in the Cains as early as July 4th, and that the large, late runs have been ocurring earlier over the years. The Cains is most famous for its canoeing. It is a gentle stream and easy to canoe, with a hauling-out place at its mouth in the village of Howards.

The sport of canoeing has grown considerably in recent years. The adventurer can float through heavily wooded rolling hills and abandoned farmlands. Beckoning salmon pools, reachable only by canoe, are waiting to be tested. And fresh salmon cooked over an open fire at streamside can satisfy even the heartiest appetite. New Brunswick's Department of Tourism has established picnic sites, tenting areas and trailer parks on rivers like the Dungarvon, The Cains and the Northwest Miramichi.

For the nonresident angler, guides can be acquired at any of the six ranger stations along the Miramichi-Nashwaak trail (Route 8), as well as outfitter information and river maps showing public waters and roadways.

Little Southwest Miramichi. (Photo by Guy Aube)

TWO
Life Cycle of the Salmon

Marr Lodge

My sons and I were standing on a ledge overlooking the Palisade pool, a thundering stretch
of rapids on the North Pole Stream. For years
we had made our annual pilgrimage to this
place. The stream is a tributary of the Little Southwest
Miramichi and is designated catch-and-release water. It
was the day after a heavy rain and the water was very high
and frightening as it spilled over the ledges in front of us,
making hollow freshet sounds.

As we watched, a large salmon attempted to jump the
falls. It made several tries and the boys kept count (five
... six ... seven). Every time the fish was about to make
it over the brink, the strong water pushed it back into the
deep whirlpool at the base of the falls. With determination
and persistence it tackled the six-foot spill, each time with
a bit more vigour (nine ... ten ... eleven). Finally, the big
beautiful fish, silver and gold in the sun, caught in the
extreme brink and held itself, struggling for traction,
fanning its tail in the face of that frothing and thundering
cascade of white water. Then it went over the top and was
gone upstream. We broke into applause. This was nature
at one of her finest moments, as well as a great lesson for
us on the endurance of this great fish and its ability to

follow the cycle established by its ancestry and get to its home spawning grounds. I prayed that it would make it all the way.

Described by experienced anglers as the best game fish in the world, the salmon faces long odds against following its life cycle and making it, unmolested, to the falls. The incidental catch of a high seas fishery, the chemicals and poisons of industrial waste, the hidden and illegal nets set in the river's estuary, the poachers' jig hooks, the native food fishery, the anglers' fly-hooks and the extremely low and warm water of a clear-cut watershed are just a few of the obstacles in its path. Certainly, human greed and government priorities of economic growth at the expense of the environment have left a great many such species extinct. Each of the aforementioned user groups must share the responsibility of protecting this great fish.

The Atlantic salmon (*Salmo salar*) is said to be worth several times the value on the fly rod than at the market place. For the angler, the salmon provides a challenge unequalled in sports fishing. While salmon has no equal on a dinner plate, memories of fishing thrills are revived time and time again when yarns are swapped at firesides.

The Miramichi drainage system offers many gravel shoals, deep-twisting eddies and giant boulders, which, combined with the frothing, sweeping currents of cold, pure water, provide the proper environment for this cold-water species. But salmon do not feed in such waters; they return here only to spawn. The Atlantic salmon spends a good deal of its lifetime feeding in the ocean. It is in the salt water that the salmon grows to its plump, snowshoe-like shape. Sometimes these fish venture as far north as the east coast of Greenland before returning to their river of birth for the November spawn. It is said that they return to within yards of their birthplace.

By spawning time the male has grown a hook on its lower jaw (thus the name *hook bill*). He is the territorial protector, claiming the spawning female against less dominant males. Before spawning, the female salmon lays on her side in a fixed position and fans her tail, creating currents that wash a nest in the gravel. She does this until the nest is 8 - 16 inches deep. Then she lays her eggs. The male, hovering nearby, extracts a milk-like substance called milt which contains sperm to fertilize the eggs. Then the female covers the spawn with gravel.

For every pound the female weighs, approximately 7,000-8,000 eggs are produced, depending on stocks and conditions; a ten-pound salmon could thus produce up to 80,000 eggs. When the water begins to warm in April or May of the following spring, the cycle continues through the various stages of development. The spawn go into an eyed-egg stage, then hatch as sac fry; the hatch rate is approximately 60 per cent. As they continue to grow, from sac fry to fingerling to parr to smolt, the survival rate declines to around three or four percent. Fewer still survive to return to their mother stream to spawn. Predators in the early stages include eels, trout and suckers. When they reach the fingerling and parr stages, fish-feeding birds like mergansers reduce their numbers further.

Salmon stocks born in a given river remain there, in fresh water, until they have grown into parr (about six inches in length) before returning to the sea. They come back three or more years later as grilse (salmon less than 25 inches in length) or salmon. Generally, a run of adult salmon is followed by a run of grilse, which in the Miramichi are mostly male. It is interesting to note that different stretches of the same river may support different salmon stocks.

After spawning, both males and females remain in the river, under the winter ice, until spring, when they are carried out to the ocean by the spring runoff. These fish are then known as black salmon. They are very thin and hungry at this time and easy to catch.

When the fish return as bright salmon, the size does not always indicate the age, but more the quality of the feeding grounds where they have spent their time. A particular salmon could weigh 12 pounds and only be three or four years old, whereas another of the same age could be considerably smaller. The actual age of a salmon can be determined by examining one of its scales (in the same fashion as we do the trunk of a tree), which under a microscope resembles a thumb print.

It is somewhat of a mystery why the returning fish rise to the fly. One theory is that it is done for recreation. But salmon are leapers, and when they are leaping they are in a state of mind to be on the move. When they are moving, or in a leaping mood, they will seldom, if ever, rise for the fly. I personally don't believe the recreational theory. Others claim that adult salmon, having spent the first years of their lives as fingerling and parr feeding in fresh water before going to the sea, will take a fly on impulse, from old feeding habits. No one has ever found food in the stomach of a spawning salmon. It is believed they take the fly, but quickly release it.

The angler either fishes from a canoe or wades into the rushing water so that a line can be cast to the salmon-holding area. Generally, these are areas where the water is swift and contains more oxygen: sometimes near springs or the mouth of entering brooks, or maybe behind a submerged rock. An artificial fly is presented in lifelike movements on the water's surface until a hit-and-move action, mimicking various insect hatches, is perfected. The lure of this insect should attract the impulsive salmon to strike. Water temperature plays an important role in this, as does the water colour and, of course, the fly pattern. These unknown variables make the hunt more of a challenge, and the eventual capture more rewarding.

Personally, I have always believed in the impulse theory: presentation over pattern. Many don't agree with this, however. But whatever science you use, a selection of fly-hooks is necessary.

There are low-water flies such as the Bear Hair, Blue Charm and Britain Grub, and high-water flies such as the Black Ghost, Mickey Finn (both streamers) and the General Practitioner. There are slow-water flies such as the Ingalls Butterfly and the Rat-faced McDougall. There are dry flies such as the Wulff series and the Bombers. There are the bugs, which can be fished either wet or dry, such as the Green Machine. A tackle shop owner or an experienced angler can help a beginning fisherman build a collection for the different conditions.

Salmon angling has been called the "Sport of Kings." Thus, for the river people, the Atlantic salmon is indeed a valuable resource. Many of us depend on the salmon for our own livelihood. As well as enjoying the recreation of fly-fishing, we work as guides, caretakers, outfitters, cooks and at many other spin-off jobs related to the fishery. We are not only concerned for its survival, but we also want to see the species thrive. We believe that hook-and-release is the answer. Personally, I release all female fish, small or large, and I seldom kill a male anymore.

When the angler has hooked a salmon or grilse and realizes that the fish is either too large to keep or that it is a female grilse that they wish to release, every precaution should be taken to ensure the fish survives. It is very easy to overtire or drown the fish by hurrying it through the water so that it cannot breathe. Adding pressure to the line may force the fish free, although breaking the leader and leaving the hook in the fish's mouth is not recommended.

When the fish is landed, quickly remove the hook and get the fish back into the water as soon as possible, without touching its gills. You should take the fish to where the water is moving (not a backwater or stagnant pond) and hold it in the water by the tail, facing into the current, until it is breathing evenly and jerking for freedom. Then release it.

*Palisade Pool on the North Pole Stream, a tributary of the
Little Southwest Miramichi River. (Photo by Guy Aube)*

THREE
Protecting a Threatened Resource

Buck Bug

I t has been said that in Colonial times a man could stand on a large rock above the water's surface at the top of the Wild Cat Pool on the Northwest Miramichi River and spear a winter's supply of salmon for the community in a single evening. Salmon were served from salt barrels in the lumber camps and even used as fertilizer by the river's farmers. Sometimes they were traded to sea captains for kegs of rum. That there would always be an abundance of salmon on the Miramichi was taken for granted.

French governor Nicolas Denys was granted a piece of land here in the year 1648, which extended from the Caspé Peninsula to the Canso Straight. He set up a trading establishment in Miramichi. Richard Denys, Sieur de France, Nicholas's son, established Fort Fronsac in 1671 and built himself a stone house near Flett's Cove in Nelson. He wrote of the salmon in Miramichi: "So great a quantity of them enters this river that at night, one is unable to sleep, so great is the noise they make in falling upon the water after having thrown or darted themselves into the air."

Robert Cooney wrote, in his 1832 history of New Brunswick and the Gaspé, about William Davidson and

Protecting a Threatened Resource

John Cort (the first Scotsmen to arrive in Miramichi, in 1765): "Here, about the year 1772 or 1773, Davidson and Cort set a cross net with which they annually caught from fourteen to eighteen hundred tierces (tierce = 300 pounds) of salmon." Such exploitation of this natural resource encouraged Benjamin Marston, the district's first sheriff, to write in 1785: "Unless the salmon fishery of this river is attended to by governments, it will be ruined by the ignorance and avarice of those conceived in it."

Sheriff Marston had foresight: our salmon stocks are in decline, the resource is threatened. Man's greed and his instinct to kill have been as ruinous to the salmon as to other exploited resources. We have eroded the fish's environment through water pollution, acid rain, the depletion of the ozone layer and extensive industrial clear-cutting (which has caused fast runoffs followed by extremely low and warm water conditions in early summer and, in many rivers, silt build-up in the spawning grounds). The resource continues to be exploited by poaching. But fish management programs and the constant surveillance by wardens, guides and anglers, as well as the educating of our young, have helped to protect this endangered species.

Other rivers in other lands have not been so fortunate. The domain of the Atlantic salmon in former times was vast in North America. They inhabited rivers along the eastern seaboard from Chesapeake Bay in the south to Ungava Bay in the north and beyond. They ran west as far as Niagara Falls. Rivers that flow into Lake Ontario, such as the Mississauga, were noted salmon streams of the day. As the rivers in the more industrial centres fell victim to mill dams, divided water courses, sawdust, factory effluence, hydro power plants and over-fishing, they were lost as salmon rivers. Salmon will not return to rivers other than their natal stream; once the river is blocked to its returning salmon runs, those fish stocks are lost forever.

In North America, the Atlantic salmon have been pressed to the extreme northeastern region of the continent. Save for one or two supporting rivers in Maine, Canada's Atlantic provinces have become a last stronghold of this species, their free-running streams relatively untainted by sewage and airborne pollution. But while the Miramichi River is today producing respectable salmon catches by modern standards, it has not been without setbacks. At times during its more recent history, disaster to its stocks loomed near in tributaries such as the Northwest.

Aerial spraying with DDT from 1952 through 1957 to control the spruce budworm outbreak in the general vicinity of the Northwest Miramichi headwaters proved disastrous to delicate salmon parr. DDT was applied at rates of half a pound per acre and is known to have caused up to 90 per cent mortality in fry and parr populations in the headwater regions.

In 1960 the spawning migration of salmon in the Northwest branch was affected by copper and zinc pollution. An old base metal mine was reopened on the Tomogonops River, a tributary of the Northwest. The mine had been used in the mid-fifties but was closed in 1958. When the mine was reopened in 1960, a large amount of water was pumped from the shaft into the tributary. This resulted in heavy-metal pollution, causing large numbers of adult salmon to return downstream.

The premature return of these fish was discovered at a counting fence at Curvington, a community on the Northwest Miramichi. The fish were tagged and released. Out of the return-ing salmon, 31 per cent finally reascended, 7 per cent were either taken commercially in the estuary waters or angled in other tributaries and 62 per cent were never seen again. Clean-up campaigns were launched and soon that tributary was flowing clean again.

Angling is the only means permitted by law to catch Atlantic salmon in fresh water. This is a conservation rule, of course, as the Atlantic salmon does not feed in fresh water. Only a few will rise to the fly. It is believed that the presence of anglers on the stream is in itself a kind of policing, as these people tend to keep each other honest and accountable.

Because of the value of the resource to the New Brunswick economy and the constant depletion of stocks, all commercial netting of the species has been shut down. An angler is given a limited number of tags per licence which are to be used on the season's limit of grilse — salmon under 25 inches long (these tags vary in numbers depending on stocks). All large salmon must be released unharmed. This restriction is enforced by officials in an attempt to rebuild brood spawning stocks and restore the river's reputation for its abundance of big fish.

Concerned anglers have been instrumental in forming conservation groups. The Atlantic Salmon Federation (ASF) of St. Andrews, New Brunswick, and its affiliate on the Miramichi, the Miramichi Salmon Association (MSA), are examples of these. The ASF, the larger group, operates on a broad scale, keeping abreast of world problems such as international boundaries, high seas fisheries and the general well-being of Atlantic salmon around the world. The MSA is a more regional concern. Problems such as poaching and river pollution are often brought to the attention of governments by the MSA. They have devoted more than 40 years and considerable funds through donations, membership fees and fund-raising campaigns to the survival of the Atlantic salmon.

For the river people and for those of us who, from time to time, test our psyche against that of the great fish, we have an obligation to see that their domain is protected and that the fish survive. Ernest Hemingway could have been thinking of the Atlantic salmon when he wrote: "For he, in all his greatness and glory is a friend. There is no one worthy of eating him, from the manner of his behaviour and great dignity."

Little Southwest Miramichi. (Photo by Guy Aube)

FOUR
A Few Words on Tackle

Oriole
Courtesy of W.W. Doak and Sons Ltd.

I won't attempt to tell the reader what to buy for tackle. I will only relate some experiences I have had in my 40-odd years of angling for salmon and trout.

My first salmon rod was a three-piece Monique Sunbeam; a nine-foot split bamboo. It was very heavy, with steel furrells, and came in a cloth sack with an extra tip. Harold Campbell, who lived across the river from home, didn't own a rod then so he and I fished together, taking turns with my rod. It seemed the tips were always breaking where they went into the furrell. So we carried a stick of furrell cement, a knife, pliers and a box of matches. When a tip broke, we would make a small fire on the shore, burn out the furrell, scrape down the tip's butt end, apply the heated cement and pushed the tip back into the furrell. Then we would run the furrell through our hair to oil it, put the rod back together and keep on fishing. Eventually the furrells would lose their temper from all the heatings and start to bend and buckle when they slipped out of place in a cast. While I still own a Thomas bamboo rod, it's a keepsake only and seldom fished with anymore.

Like everyone who fished then, I eventually graduated to a fibreglass rod, which was lighter, stronger and much more practical. I have an eight-foot, ten-inch fibreglass Fenwick which is also retired after much abuse and several fish. Now I use an eight-foot American-made sage-graphite rod. Boron and graphite, by fibreglass and bamboo standards, are weightless and trouble-free. Personally, I prefer a rod with a good backbone, as this seems to give me more leverage to pick line off the water and enables me to cast a bit further in bad conditions (although this doesn't always hold true). It also seems to give me a faster and more sensitive touch in setting the hook when a fish strikes. Stiff rods play fish quicker, which is important if you intend to release them.

The beginning angler should start with basic equipment. I would recommend starting off with a low-end graphite or boron rod. They are in the $100 price range and can be purchased at any tackle shop. Good names to look for are Scott, Sage, Fenwick, Winston, Loomis and Orvis. If the beginner is still interested in the sport after a season or two, that would be the time to purchase the more expensive rod.

However, everyone should own a good reel; that is, one that will hold at least 100 yards of backing and the casting line without being so crowded you have no room on the spindle when your line gets wet. The reel should also balance properly with the rod. My first reel was made by J.W. Young. At the time, they were making two popular salmon reels: the Condex and the Pridex. Mine was a Condex, which held up all through my boyhood and my teen years. It was eventually stolen from my father's old cabin. I don't know if J.W. Young still has that same reputation for quality.

Reels come and go like any fad in clothing or sporting goods; sometimes it may be popular to have a certain make. In the 1960s everyone on the river was using the quiet, American-made Phleuger model. Phleuger made a variety of sizes with two-inch, three-inch and four-inch spools. One model had a ring in front for the line to go through. I once had this model, but I sold it after losing a big salmon because I had assembled my tackle in a hurry and neglected to put the line through the ring. Instead, the line came off the reel through the V under the ring and the splice between my backing and casting line jammed in the V and the leader broke. But this was no fault of the Phleuger people and their reels

29

remained popular. In fact, there were even imitations of the Phleuger which were made in Japan. They looked the same at a distance but were of poor quality. Their screws fell out, their dowels bent and they jammed and twisted in their frames. Their handles fell off, the drag-set buttons quit functioning and they backlashed. I think Phleuger's reputation also diminished toward the end of its popularity. Maybe it was due to the mass production required to supply the demand or perhaps it was just the nature of the fad. After that we all criticized Phleuger openly. It was the popular thing to do.

I then purchased a British-made Hardy, which I am still using today. Hardy makes many models. Among these are the Saint John, Saint George, Marquis and Hardy Perfect. I have the Marquis, which seems just the right balance for my eight-foot graphite. The Hardy reel offers no frills, but it is expensive and durable, and will outlive us all. The Hardy also has a loud drag, which some people like. This I could live without.

My friend Doug Underhill fishes with a reel made by the Valentine people, who own a lodge on the Cains River. Their reel is gear-driven, which means that for every turn you make on the handle, two or three go onto the spindle. These are good for picking up line fast when you are forced to gather the slack as a salmon is running toward you.

My son Jeff fishes with an Orvis Batten Kill reel, which is popular right now among anglers. Orvis has a reputation for quality in fishing tackle which is second to none in North America. However, their reels are not expensive.

But the reel I have always dreamed of owning and could never afford is the Bogdon. This is a handmade, durable, wide-spindled, double-cranked piece of steel, made in New England by Mr. Stan Bogdon. He has a waiting list three years long. The Bogdon reel has become a lasting fad among our American friends.

There are many names in reels and only a few that I have had experience with. Companies like Shakespeare, Fenwick, Diwa and Scientific Angler produce top-quality products. If you are a novice angler looking for a reel, it is best to consult your local tackle shop owner. This professional will show you an inexpensive but durable reel and balance it properly on your rod. You can't get this kind of expertise in a department store or serve-yourself outlet; it certainly isn't available in a mail-order catalogue.

As important as a rod and reel are, they would not benefit you if you were lost in the wilderness or facing starvation. But if you had a hook and a piece of line, you could catch fish in the pockets of small streams. Hence, these are the most important parts of your tackle.

With my first outfit, I had a "level" line, which was common at the time. "Level" meant that it was the same size all the way along. As the front end became worn and cracked, a piece was cut off. Eventually the line became very short. In fact, I can recall fishing with a casting line so short that when I made a long cast, the splice between it and the backing would rattle its way out through the rod guides. One good thing about this, however, was the way I could shoot the heavier casting line to great distances. That is, if I could keep the small backing untangled in my hand. Sometimes I think that this is the way the weight-forward and the torpedo-tapered lines were invented. But these lines were never for me, and because of my aforementioned agonies with bad casting lines, I have not been able to use them to this day.

I now use a double tapered line, and I am in a small minority. The average fly-fisher, and certainly the novice angler, uses the weight-forward lines. They shoot easier and, unless you plan to cast 50 or so feet of line, there is not a pick-up problem nor is there a tangle problem with the line's smallness back of the taper. So it is probably the most practical line to use. For reasons that are perhaps philosophical, I've stayed with the double taper line. I use the Cortland #444 in sizes 8, 9 or 10, whichever works best on the particular rod I'm using. Sometimes I use Scientific Angler, who also make an excellent fly line. Proper balance in fly lines is a personal matter. It would be impossible to list all the lines suitable for a given rod.

With double taper lines, once you are comfortable casting half of the 30 yards of its length, you are handling the big part of the line, which is much less likely to tangle in your hands or in the boat or water beside you. Nobody really needs a shooting taper to cast 15 yards. If you want to reach a great distance, you still have the most shootable portion of the line to work with. Remember

KNOTS

	Leader Knot *ends go opposite way*
	Wedge Knot *leader to line*
	Passing leader through loop
	Tying leader to straight hook
	Tying leader to turned up or turned down eye
	Casting line to backing: fray, knot, wrap and polish

Guide Roy Curtis, Ted Williams and Wayne Curtis.

also that the long cast is not always the right cast and that accuracy is what is most important. I have fished behind long casters and have caught salmon in the waters between them and their fly-hook. Also, with double tapers, when the front half starts to wear, I swing it end for end, which gives the line twice the life. My friend Harold, who started out fishing with me, and who suffered many of the same aggravations, still uses the double taper and swears by it. These are only personal preferences, however, and are to be treated accordingly. You should use what is most comfortable and works the best for your particular circumstance.

When I am fishing regularly, I like to dress my line every day. A line will rot and crack from the dirt it picks up in the water. When you go over your line with the proper dressing, you will notice a black greasy film accumulating on the wool pad you're dressing with. This is the dirt the line picks up from the water. Insect repellent contains solvents that will ruin a casting line. Also, a line not dressed or dried out occasionally will get water-logged and hard to manage.

For backing, fish twine or a small braided nylon line such as the type used for bait fishing is sufficient. The smaller this line is, the better. Most tackle shops carry spools of the proper fine nylon backing, which is about 20 pounds test and inexpensive. Your pound test should be greater than that of your leader. It is wise to carry all the backing your reel will hold. It will come in handy if you hook a big fish in the big river.

To splice your casting line to the backing there are many methods. I use the old-fashioned splice, which is safe and easy on the rod guides. I scrape the cover from the casting line down to the core back about two inches from the end. I make a square knot between it and the backing, then wrap the whole concern with a fine thread, an inch or so each way from the knot. When the splice is wrapped smooth, I varnish and let it dry. This splice is seldom through the rod guides other than when playing a big fish, so it will outlive the line itself.

Of all the revolutions that have taken place in fishing tackle, the greatest has been in fly-hooks. In the early fifties and for many years before, everyone was fishing with the Scottish pattern flies: the Silver Doctor, Jack Scott, Black Dose and Silver Grey. The exceptions to these were perhaps the Red Squirrel Tail or Black Bear Hair patterns. We had been led to believe that a fly-hook should have a dozen different colours and that, if it didn't, it would mean the difference between success and failure.

The late Everett Price (the best fly-tier I ever knew) owned a small fly-tying shop in Blackville. I spent a lot of time hanging out there. I would take him hen, duck and turkey feathers in exchange for fly-hooks. My favourite fly in those days was the Oriole, and Mr. Price was the last man I knew that could tie one properly. He gave me a good many and I fished with them regularly and with great success. The Oriole had a black body and hackle, a Golden Pheasant underwing and tail and green Mallard feathers "roofed" for the main wing. Whenever Mr. Price gave me an Oriole, he would say, "Now don't touch this fly until you fish it." Once the fly-hook was fished, the wings would stay in their roofed position. People in the community associated me with the Oriole fly-hook and, indeed, it was a boyhood friend to me. Years later, when I built my own lodge on the river, I named it Camp Oriole. (It has since become the meeting place for the Oriole Anglers Club, a group of 25 Canadian anglers. We pool our membership to lease new waters and to rebuild some traditions in angling that seemed to be slipping away.)

In any event, fly-hooks were very personal and important things to us then. A kind of confidence came with owning and fishing a certain pattern. One day, when I had no Oriole flies, I went fishing with a Squirrel Tail and got three grilse. After that, I gained confidence in that hook, which I could tie myself.

But fly-hooks went from one extreme to the other with the invention of the Ingalls Butterfly. Where they were once closely copied traditional patterns, they became widely varied patterns with hair wings and exaggerated imitations. I can remember fishing that fly-hook for the first time. Maurice Ingalls, the fly's inventor, had an outfit of camps on the Miramichi River about four miles from home in the area of Ted Williams's Swinging Bridge pool. But Mr. Ingalls owned no water and his campers fished everywhere. They were at our place some of the time. One day, when Maurice was at our shore with his guests, he gave me his newly invented Butterfly hook and I reluctantly tied it onto the leader before going out in the canoe alone. When I had anchored the canoe on the opposite side of the run, I took off the Butterfly and tied on an Oriole. After I had hooked and landed two grilse, Ingalls yelled, "I told you so!" Not wanting to hurt his feelings, I took the Oriole off and put his fly back on the leader before going to shore. Ingalls wanted one of the fish.

But we all had to learn to fish the new, and often gaudy, patterns. Today we are catching fish with flies that we would have been laughed off the river for using 30 years ago. It helps to strengthen my theory of presentation over pattern, and that salmon take flies on impulse.

Some types of flies are wet, dry, high and low water, slow and fast water, bright and dirty water, bugs, bombers, stone fly nymphs, flies to match various insect hatches, and streamers, which are imitations of small fish. A small selection is all you need. The most productive at any given time is the best seller at the tackle shop.

If you are not from the Miramichi and wonder when to go fishing, you can probably go to school on what the local river people tell you. These people are nearer to the river than anyone and are in tune with the way the salmon are thinking, which side of the river the fish are running, what hook they are taking and how the hook should be presented. You can always tell if the fish are running by the number of locals on the river. River folk won't waste time fishing if there are no fish running. These are working people: woodsmen, truck drivers, farmers, mechanics, teachers and mill workers. When they go fishing it's to catch a fish for the table as well as for a bit of leisure. As long as the word of mouth is "No fish up yet," they do other things and save their river time for when the run is on. The river could be full of strangers and it wouldn't mean a thing. Jack Sullivan, the flamboyant outfitter who operated an outfit of camps in Blissfield until his death, used to ask people, "Do ya live here, or do ya fish?"

FIVE
Wallace W. Doak and Sons: Steeped in Tradition

Thunder & Lightning

W. Doak and Sons, the fishing tackle business in Doaktown, New Brunswick, has come a long way since its founder, the late Wallace Doak, built his first fly-tying bench upstairs over his father's woodshed in 1929. In the 50 years that followed, Doak tied more than five thousand fly-hooks a year — an estimated quarter of a million before his death in 1979. During that time he established a tackle shop on Main Street that has become a traditional stopping place for the many anglers from all over the world who come to fish the Miramichi.

Wallace Doak was born in 1913 and raised in Doaktown. As a young man he was an avid angler. He worked as a river guide and thus developed an interest in the art of fly-tying. He learned his craft from observing other fly-tiers, reading books on the subject and practising for countless hours. He offered his flies to the fishermen he was guiding. Doak was a meticulous man by nature and soon became an excellent tier; his flies were used everywhere. They were always tied according to pattern and durability. More importantly, they caught fish.

Wallace had his own theory on fly-tying. He never tried to be an inventor, but kept with the belief that there

Wallace W. Doak and Sons: Steeped in Tradition

(Left) Doak's original tackle shop, built in 1946, on Main Street in Doaktown.

(Right) Wallace Doak in his shop.

were enough fly patterns on the market and certainly more demand for traditional patterns than he could supply. He felt that it was important for a commercial fly-tier to have a reputation for consistency of pattern and quality. Customers knew, as they came back year after year, that they could always find the same patterns, tied in the same way.

Wallace's first business outlet was the upstairs of his father's woodshed. Here, he fashioned a tier's bench of boards and built himself a desk. It was said that when Wallace Doak wasn't on the river, he was at his bench. At this time, the family lived down the South Road, a short distance from Doaktown. In the evenings, customers would drive to the Doak home for flies.

His first wholesale business began when he started to sell flies to W.R. McLosky, the large general store in Boiestown, 17 miles up the river. Doak delivered his shipments of flies to McLosky by bicycle. Later, when he had purchased a car, he made regular deliveries to James S. Neil & Sons, a sporting goods store in Fredericton.

In 1945, Wallace married and built a home on Main Street in Doaktown. The following year, he built a little shop on the corner of his front lawn. It was here that his fly-tying became a full-time business. He also kept the shop stocked with everything an angler would need in the way of tackle. The sign hanging over the sidewalk read W.W. Doak — Fishing Tackle.

Wallace Doak was a devout Christian and ran the shop with a few basic rules: offer quality product for the money, regard all customers (rich or poor) as simply fishermen and treat them equally, and don't allow profane language in the shop. This, combined with Mr. Doak's personality, proved to be a successful formula. As respect for the man grew, so did the business. Fishermen who went into the shop for tackle were considered friends first and customers second.

When Wallace Doak died in 1979, his son Jerry, who grew up in the business, took over the shop. Jerry is proud of his father's philosophy.

Doak's new tackle shop.

Wallace W. Doak and Sons: Steeped in Tradition

"Dad had a deep sense of personal and professional integrity. He had a very strong concept of fair treatment for all customers, regardless of their station in life or the amount of money in their pocket," Jerry said. "When a customer came into the shop, they were simply 'All fishermen' to Dad." In October 1983, Wallace Doak became the first fly-tier to be inducted into the Atlantic Salmon Hall of Fame at the Salmon Museum in Doaktown. Since then, Jerry has moved the business to a new location down the street, expanded the quarters and established a successful catalogue service. The shop now employs a staff of three, as well as several outside fly-tiers. Jerry is a conservationist and a director of the Miramichi Salmon Association. Wallace's other son, George, operates a tackle business in Fredericton. Indeed, the Doak family has become a tradition in New Brunswick fly-fishing.

SIX
Steve's Tackle Shop

Rusty Rat

"*T here, where the rapids churn and roar, and the ice flows bellowing run; where the tortured, twisted rivers of blood rush to the setting sun — I've packed my grip and I'm going boys, 'ere another day is done." - Robert W. Service*

The lure of our beautiful streams and forests is inspiring to many red-blooded adventurers. And an almost certain stop along the way is the tackle shop, for supplies. A good tackle shop is not only a place to buy tackle and related gear, it's also a place to get advice from the shop pro on equipment and technique, to hear yarns of hunting and fishing trips and to share with other sportsmen your own experiences afield. No other business can boast of having the optimism, chivalry, exaggerations and just plain excitement that is found in the tackle shop business. Steve Allen's tackle shop in Newcastle is no exception.

At Allen's, people are mostly hustling about the store. Some are buying fishing tackle, some buying licences and others are just there to catch the excitement. Here the spirits are always high, the adrenalin flows and there is always joking and jibbing in the madness. In their eagerness, they are all hell-bent for the river, especially when the salmon are running.

Members of the staff are also jubilant. A young man may be tying flies at the vice, another moodily splicing lines behind the counter. Steve, the proprietor, is generally shouting instructions to his customers about rod sizes, fly-hook patterns and directions to the salmon pools. Indeed, there is optimism at the top of the season at the old tackle shop.

Established in 1946 by Steve's father Charles and an uncle, Leslie Allen, this shop has served a clientele of sportsmen from all corners of the continent with dedication and a knowledge of the trade plus a calibre of yarn-swapping unavailable beyond the Miramichi. Steve's mother, Florence Allen, has worked in the store since 1959. Steve's many years of experience as a hunter, angler, outfitter and guide, combined with his colourful personality, have been his biggest assets in building a successful tackle business. Steve knows the best type of hunting and fishing supplies anyone would need.

Since 1926, when Steve's grandfather, Alfred, established a fishing camp on the Little Southwest Miramichi River, the area has been a scene of many hunting and fishing adventures. The cabin can boast of its heritage of thrilling anecdotes. There are camp logs which have been kept for generations.

Steve's father, the late Charlie Allen, recorded shooting a white deer in 1935: "A natural albino . . . spikehorn with pink eyes." It was said that they hunted for trophy racks in those days, and small bucks and does were passed up. One November afternoon in 1952, Charles recorded shooting two trophy-size bucks, filling his licence. Each had a spread of antlers exceeding 22 inches.

As well as being a registered New Brunswick guide, Steve is a member of a conservation group, the Miramichi Salmon Association. He feels a responsibility to conserve wildlife and to protect sportsmen's interests for the future. For this, he is looked upon as a model sportsman, and the fame of his angling guests are widely known. At one time, the Allens were host to jazz musician Benny Goodman, an avid salmon angler.

At the shop, everyone is treated with the same consideration, from the humble river guide in search of a decent raincoat to the "big time" sportsman displaying all the earmarks of a rich Ameri-

Steve Allen in his Newcastle shop.

can on vacation. Locals can rub elbows with a member of the prestigious New York Anglers Club, sports announcer Kurt Gowdy or t.v.'s Red Fisher. Here, at the river, such name sportsmen share a bond with the locals. All are in pursuit of the Atlantic salmon, all are seeking just the right feather or string of yarn that will help bring in the "big one." As part of his work, Steve listens to the yarns of boisterous braggarts, claiming the impossible . . . and relates to every tale, occasionally adding a finishing touch. He can be found comforting weary Nimrods, returning with tales of woe and lamenting the big one that got away.

If everyone at the shop is busy, browsing can be entertaining. Local anglers George Hubbard, Pat Underhill or Grissley Galliah may be pondering over some pattern flies in a showcase. The hooks may look like twins at first glance, but a closer look will reveal that each has a different feather.

A tale might be heard, like that of a guide from far up the river who claims, "Boys, the salmon are bitin' sa good at my pool, ya have ta hide behind a tree to tie on yer fly-hook." Such a claim would send up a brief chuckle about the shop. An elderly man might approach the counter to inquire, "What are they taking this year, Stevie?" Steve might reply, "Just about anything you throw in the river." But he would probably pass the man a box containing variations of the Ingalls Butterfly, fresh off the vice; the best selling fly-hook in the shop.

An old guide might be heard telling of a moose hunt, where the moose were so scarce that another guide had to be posted in the hills to answer his calls. Or he might tell of guiding the famous moose hunter who complained bitterly about his choice of a lake. Keeping his guest happy, the guide walked him about the hills, getting him lost and returning him to the same lake, at which the guest shouted, "Ah! A bigger lake and a better lake!" Here, of course, they would soon get a moose.

Possibly, the next best thing to being in the out-of-doors is being at the old tackle shop.

SEVEN
The Famous Butterfly

Butterfly

*T*he late Jack Sullivan was an outfitter and river guide who lived in the small community of Blissville on the Miramichi River. During the angling season he hosted guests in his farmhouse and adjacent cabins, generally nonresident fly-fishers who came to the Miramichi in search of the Atlantic salmon. Guiding their rushing canoes through the churning rapids and across the gleaming lakes of the Miramichi was a way of life for Sullivan. He loved the field work and, like a scout leader at camp, he preached conservation and the ethics of outdoor sports. He taught many a novice adventurer the ways of the river, how to handle a canoe, cast a fly, camp in the wilderness. Spirited campfire songs, the singing of spinning reels and the splash of a battling salmon were familiar sounds to the outfitter.

But the angling season of the northeast is short-lived. Bumping ice flows crowd the rivers immediately following the October fishery, sending the river people hustling south. The country becomes barren as the river freezes above the spawning salmon. The beautiful summits along the river bank, visited by passing canoeists throughout the angling season, are now silent. The hush is broken only by the hammering woodpecker or the scream of a whiskey-jack.

To an outfitter and guide like Sullivan, the long winter season until the spring breakup in mid-April meant several months without the work he loved. Over the years, Sullivan tried his hand at various jobs at lumber camps, sawmills and construction sites. But some 20 years ago, he found a hobby in fly-tying. During the winter months he produced quantities of salmon flies for fishermen up and down the Atlantic seaboard. Some of the fly patterns tied at Sullivan's cabin were called Bugs, Bombers, Rat-faces, Wulff's, Nymphs and Streamers. But the most common in the shop was the Ingalls Butterfly.

The Butterfly was invented in the early 1960s by American Maurice Ingalls. He was an old crony of Sullivan's and stayed for a time at the latter's cabin. Once an outfitter on the Miramichi River himself, Ingalls kept a guest camp in what is now known as the Ted Williams's Swinging Bridge pool area. That's where he put together the first stages of the Butterfly. It's a slow-water hook and was designed for the big Southwest Miramichi River, at the Ingalls camp. Having learned the hook pattern and its potential first-hand, Sullivan began tying Butterflies for anglers in the United States and Canada. Local anglers could acquire both the Butterfly and variations of the original design at general stores and service stations throughout the Miramichi valley.

The original stages of the pattern consisted of a black yarn body on a number 5 hook and two 45-degree angle wings of white goat hair. The flexible wings would gyrate through the water when retrieved properly. The movement mimics the motions of a water bug or a swimming insect. Sullivan claimed that Ingalls had fished the basic Butterfly successfully for many years before releasing word of his invention. During that time, Ingalls experimented. Eventually he presented the idea to Wallace Doak, of W.W. Doak & Sons tackle shop in Doaktown. Doak agreed that the pattern showed promise, but he changed the body from black yarn to a peacock herl and added brown hackle feathers. The Ingalls Butterfly was born.

Seasoned salmon anglers on the Miramichi River were initially reluctant to try the strange-looking hook. Having used the more conservative feathered classics successfully, they frowned on the ugly Butterfly. But the pattern was not to be denied its place in the angling world, and soon it appeared in showcases and tackle boxes, pushing aside many old patterns.

On the rivers, the Ingalls Butterfly was catching salmon in almost all conditions and, as word of its capabilities swept the salmon world, the demand grew. Distributors, fly-tiers, shop-keepers, outfitters and river guides, as well as the anglers, sought out the pattern. Anglers enjoyed a sense of confidence with the Butterfly as its catch average went beyond that of any other salmon fly in history. For the tackle shop owner it was a commodity offering high turnover and quick profits. For the fly-tier like Sullivan, it kicked off an era known as the "Butterfly boom."

After the Ingalls years, Sullivan tied many thousands of Butterflies, some of which are variations of the original pattern. They are now tied to hooks of various sizes with multicoloured bodies. They have slim or large bodies for slow and fast water, respectively. In fast water, the large body gives the hook the appearance of a nymph as the heavy current closes the wings. As a result of the boom, goat hair has become very scarce and many shop owners have had to substitute white hair from other domestic farm animals to create the distinctive wings of the fly.

While anglers in eastern Canada and the United States reviewed their inventory of fly-hooks for the spring season, in Sullivan's small cabin the wood stove would keep a steady heat as the smoke pipe creaked and rattled in the wind. I can picture the man at his work while winter rages outside: Sullivan crouched over an ancient roll-top desk, its drawers jammed with coloured yarn, hooks, thread and a thousand feathers; Sullivan fortified with tobacco and coffee, carefully wrapping yarn around a bare hook, his plaid shirt, suspenders and drooped moustache marking him as a river-man. On the desk, to his right, a cigar box containing hundreds of Butterflies. Like so many insects, they would have a short life expectancy: some retired to fly cases, never to be used again after taking trophy-sized Atlantic salmon, others to be traded among the anglers who swap flies at the river's edge as they exchange fishing tales.

Although the rewards may seem small, fly-tying for Sullivan was a hobby that kept him at the summer camp all year long. That was reward enough.

EIGHT
Lost at the Net

Pink Lady

*A*s a boy growing up on the Miramichi in the fifties, organized sports were beyond my reach, so I practised fly-casting the way a city youngster works on a tennis serve or golf swing. There were always American sportsmen staying at our camp; men who were scientific in their approach and inevitably owned the very best and the very latest equipment. Sometimes they would spin yarns for my benefit, all about the different rivers they had visited, the many mighty fish they had defeated and the mightier fish that had defeated them. There was the Beaverkill for brown trout, the Colorado for steelhead and the Eagle, Whale, Matane and Restigouche for Atlantic salmon. Frequent references were made to their mentors, men like Lee Wulff, Art Flick, Kurt Gowdie and others. Later in life I discovered that some of these very men had developed similar reputations themselves.

Sometimes these same guests would give me the full-dressed and very expensive Scottish pattern fly-hooks of that day, which I would graciously accept and tie on the leader in their presence. But when their backs were turned, I would replace the rainbow-coloured wonders with the squirrel patterns I had tied myself at a bench in the back warehouse of my father's store. The expensive patterns were safely stored away, to be copied later.

The guests also offered advice on technique and equipment. Back then, my own tackle consisted of a split bamboo Monique rod, a simple reel from the Eaton's catalogue, and a level casting line with net twine for backing. The Americans easily out-cast me by 20 yards. Still, with my knowledge of the home pool and the river in general, I was able to hold my own among them, and they afforded me status as an equal (at least on my turf).

Sometimes I even out-fished the better-equipped visitors, much to the chagrin of the guides, and I would be admonished by my father to stay out of the pool when the sports were there! My fishing time was limited to periods when the guests were off the river, perhaps in camp having lunch or a midday break. So much for high-end equipment and the scientific approach.

One breezy September day, while the guests were in camp having lunch and the guides were huddled by a fire on the gravel bar, I hooked a large salmon. The guides cheered me on as I fought the big fish, leading it downstream to where they were to give assistance with its landing. It was a very large salmon, a Cains River hookbill weighing well over 20 pounds.

One of the group, whose name I have long forgotten, picked up a landing net and offered to dip the fish for me. I accepted his offer and together we followed the fish along the gravel bar, around the bend and into some slack water until it finally tired and appeared to be ready for netting. The guide then attempted to scoop the big fish.

It immediately became obvious to me that this man knew nothing about netting a salmon. He seemed to be doing everything wrong, in contrast to the better guides I had seen netting fish. He was carrying the net high above the water, wading in after the fish and plunging the net after the salmon as it circled him, so that the line was catching up in his clothing. At one point, the big fish flopped off the net's too-small hoop. After about 20 minutes of this horrible exhibition, I lost the fish when the old casting line snapped and the salmon swam slowly away. The man was genuinely embarrassed and sorry.

That fish story grieves me to this day. Back then I knew some of the fundamentals of netting a salmon, but at that tender age I was too intimidated to instruct my older friend. Since then I have

Jeff plays salmon at Table Rock on the North Pole Stream.

learned the proper technique, partly by accident and partly by experience.

Discussion of the topic by seasoned anglers inevitably produces horror stories like my own. Today, when someone picks up a net to dip a large fish for me, I am not in the least intimidated and make fully certain that my net-minder does what I ask. When I am faced with an inept netsman, I ask him to step back and let me beach the fish.

Through the years I have found the dos and don'ts of netting fish, particularly large ones. It's surprising how many folks are out there with poorly designed or inadequately sized dip nets. Any large fish requiring two hands to lift when in the net calls for a net handle of at least four feet in length, or one that will telescope to this length. Correct hoop size is generally much larger than one might imagine and should be deep enough in its netting to contain even the largest fish. Many nets that are found in department stores are too small all around. Err on the site of bigness: too large a net will still work, too small will not. I prefer the old-fashioned iron hoop net with a wooden handle. Some anglers weight their nets with a stone, which holds the net open to the bottom, reducing the risk of tangling.

The most important rule is to recognize when a large fish is ready to come to the net, for it can be fatal to act too quickly. The accepted sign is when the fish rises to the surface from the pressure of the bowed rod. "The tail's up! He's ready!" veterans can be heard to say.

When taking your fish to shore from a wading position well out in a stream or lake, it is best to keep pressure on the fish from the side on which it was initially hooked, if possible. If you are wading, this will happen as a matter of convenience. Failure to do this can cause the hook to twist out of the mouth, since leverage will be applied contrary to how the hook was set.

Netting from a boat anchored in a moderate stream, the angler should be stationed to the stern so the netter can reach the fish. Light canoes, however, are cause for extreme caution in such circumstances. This technique should never be practised in fast or heavy currents, for standing in the anchor end while the anchor is dropped will dangerously destabilize the canoe to the extent that water could pour over the stern gunwale, sinking you in seconds. Whenever possible, the netting should take place on the opposite side of the canoe from the anchor rope. This way, the leverage of

Wayne Curtis fishing the Cains.

the taut rope will steady the canoe, the weight being redistributed from the centre to one side as the fish is landed. Pulling the anchor and paddling or polling ashore is safer when faced with an unstable boat/large fish situation. This should be done, in any event, when a large fish makes a run, as there is a risk of the fish getting under the boat or around the anchor rope.

Reaching the shore and with the fish played out, the angler should back up as high as possible along the bank and hold his rod fairly high to allow the netter to work under the line. Here the netter should stand on the downstream side of the line so the fish can be led down to him in the current. A competent netter will never wade directly into the stream, but rather, find a convenient spot where there is depth for the job to be done, and stay there, motionless. The wading netter is at a distinct disadvantage, for the fish can circle him, causing the line to tangle in clothing.

The net should be rested in the water early and left there. It is the angler's responsibility to get the fish to the net, not the netter's responsibility to get the net to the fish. Plunging a scoop net into the water at even a well-played fish will produce an additional rush of adrenalin and cause it to find new life and scoot away. Wearing bright clothing whilst netting can produce the same effect. Then again, wearing bright clothing while fishing is rarely a good idea. And no smoking please! I have seen monofilament snap almost instantly when touched by a lit cigarette.

A good angler (and an inexperienced one with the benefit of some good pointers) can lead a played fish to and over a scoop net. When the fish is approaching the net, the angler should hold the rod in such a way so as to prevent the monofilament from touching the net hoop on entry. And the netter, for his part, should ensure that the head goes into the hoop first. The bigger the fish, the more important this rule is. A fish can only swim forward. Believe it or not, I have seen people trying to scoop fish from the tail end.

When a large specimen is finally in the net, the net should never be hoisted above the water, but cradled until the fish can be lifted to shore. I've seen many a potential trophy flip to freedom and an over-jubilant netter's jaw drop when salmon went through the net.

Last year, I had the good fortune to hook a large June salmon. I brought it to the same gravel bar where I had lost a large salmon so many years before. When it seemed to be ready, and not wishing to over-stress the fish, I led it toward the waiting net in the capable hands of my friend Bob Miller. As I strained to turn his head, the hook suddenly pulled out. Almost disbelieving, I turned to walk away and hide my disappointment. But Bob was peering in the water, concentrating hard and completely unaware that I had lost the fish. Because he was using the old tried and true rules, he had scooped the salmon into the net before it had realized the hook was out!

NINE
Building the Miller Canoe

Hairy Mary

The Miller Canoe factory of New Brunswick is responsible for one of the most popular canoes ever used on the Miramichi River.

Vic Miller built his first canoe in 1925. It was a rugged boat constructed with a few hand tools in the attic of his house and lowered from the window on long poles. This first effort was crude in comparison to the standards that were later set in the canoe-building projects of the Miller family. Still, that first canoe was strong, serviceable, excellent in balance and made-to-order for the long portage roads and the turbulent rivers and lakes in this part of the country.

Today, after 60 years of canoe building, the Miller family has become known as one of the best in the business. Indeed, the Millers are offering their clients some of the finest examples of craftsmanship in the world today.

The Miller family lives outside Nictau in a farm-type setting on the banks of the Tobique River near where the Sisson Branch, Little Tobique and Mamozekel rivers join at the forks of the Tobique, a tributary of the St. John River. It was here that Vic Miller, after serving in the First World War (he was wounded while with the 26th Battalion at the Battle of Vimy Ridge), returned to his old homestead to establish a headquarters for his fishing expeditions, which would involve 50-mile river runs down the Mamozekel and the Tobique rivers from Serpentine Lake.

He leased the Serpentine Lake and River from the New Brunswick government and built fishing camps there. Vic was reputed to have an excellent awareness of the woods plus great stream savvy, and he mapped out this region (accurate to scale) on foot, finding the untested waters of the Serpentine region. Guests who have come to Nictau to take part in the fishing expeditions over the years include J.D. Rockefeller Jr., Governor Mortimer Proctor of Vermont and Mrs. Phelps (a millionaire whose husband drowned aboard the Titanic).

For Vic Miller, the canoes were built from necessity. They had to be safe and durable to carry his guests and their cargo — features the Miller canoe still has.

Today, Bill Miller Jr. is head craftsman, carrying on his grandfather's legacy to keep the Miller canoe up to its original standards. Each canoe built in the Miller shop is modelled to perfection and stamped with the family name, carrying with it a good part of the old Miller tradition as a down-home canoe company. Old Vic Miller's moulds and standards of material are still used.

The Miller canoe is built from well-seasoned lumber which is hand-picked from the woods and later edged to Miller specifications by a portable sawmill on the property. The planking and rib work is first steamed, then bowed from white cedar. White spruce is used in making the one-piece gunwales. The thwarts are carved from maple, and the seats filled with hand-woven cane. All of the tacks that hold the Miller canoe together are brass, as are the gunwale screws. All are hand-driven and clinched in such a fashion as not to weaken an area or section of lumber.

When the main structure is finished, the inside woodwork is bathed in linseed oil and eventually varnished in stages to the proper depth and gloss. The canoe exterior is covered with canvas brought in from Yarmouth, N.S., via a firm in Toronto. (This is sailing ship material and not easily acquired in these parts.) Sometimes fibreglass is used as an outside covering if requested

(Above) Canoe under construction using Miller's famous moulds.
(Below) Canoe builder Bill Miller Jr.

by a customer, but for the most part, canvas is used. "We prefer to stay with the canvas coverings," says Bill Jr. "They're quieter in the water and much more flexible on the rocks."

As well as building canoes, the Miller family also makes paddles, folding canoe seats and other accessories. These are all hand-carved from maple and birch. "We build the accessories according to demand," says Bill Jr. "If anyone wants a given size or model, we set up and build it. Most of our canoes are now built to fill special orders."

Miller has built as many as 48 canoes in a single season, as well as the accessories. "This year we built something like 16," says Bill Jr. "The recession has slowed us down somewhat. We were very busy during the seventies and early eighties."

According to Bill Miller Sr., the Chestnut Canoe people adopted a model of the Miller boat to be built at their factory in Fredericton. "It was on the Miramichi that Mr. Chestnut was fishing salmon and began to comment on the Miller canoe that his guide, a Mr. Olgilvie, was using," says Bill Sr. "Mr. Chestnut liked the boat so much that they adopted the model (which was called the Olgilvie) from Vic Miller and they were built for many years at that factory."

Over the years the Miller canoe has been made in many models, ranging from the 12-footer to the 26-foot freighter. They carry model names such as the Moore, J.D. Miller, Gallop and the Chickadee. Most of these are sold through word of mouth from happy customers who know about canoes.

In 1983, Bill Miller Jr. designed a special model as his own private Bicentennial project. He called it the Chickadee, after the provincial bird. It is a specially designed canoe with fancy hand-carved thwarts and the bird engraved on the hull. Bill is currently working on the design of a sailing canoe as well as a 15-foot white-water solo canoe which can also be used for leisure canoeing. It's called the Kingfisher.

Since the old days, when Vic Miller commenced building boats, canoes have been launched into streams from New York to California, Alaska and the Yukon. Even today a Vic Miller original is sometimes returned to the shop for repairs — up to 50 years after its construction. They have been purchased by people such as the governor of Vermont and many camp owners and outfitters across Canada, as well as by the Department of Fisheries and Natural Resources.

Indeed, Miller Canoes has become one of the most skilled boat builders in the country. To be sure, each boat is still built to perfection. Always perfection.

TEN
The Miramichi Salmon Museum

Yellow Torrish

W hen Doaktown's Miramichi Historic Society was formed in 1973, its goal was to establish an Atlantic salmon museum in the village. Such a project had been long overdue. The Miramichi being long rated as a world-class salmon river, and the Atlantic salmon having put the region on the map, the society thought it fitting to construct a salmon museum in the geographic centre of the river's fly-fishing reaches. This dream became a reality in 1982 when the federal and provincial governments awarded grants of $228,000 and $115,000 toward its construction. W.R. McKinnon, a Doaktown businessman, donated the three and a half acre riverside property where the fishing-lodge style structure overlooks a Miramichi salmon pool. In addition, $50,000 was raised through donations and local fund-raising campaigns.

The Miramichi Atlantic Salmon Museum opened in the summer of 1983. This is a unique tourist attraction, where salmon enthusiasts gather to celebrate the existence of this noble gamefish. The museum incorporates sundecks and windows that overlook the natural habitat of the Atlantic salmon. There are sandstone fences, flowerbeds and a fireplace, adding to the campsite atmosphere. There is also a smokehouse, icehouse, boathouse, woodsheds, outhouses and a guides' camp. Inside, the museum features a live display of the Atlantic salmon in an aquarium designed to show salmon development at its various stages. There is a fly-tying bench, a poachers' corner, a guide and outfitters' section, a fishing photo and film exhibit and various artifacts as well as a banquet facility for 140 people. Each year, new members are inducted into the Miramichi Salmon Hall of Fame.

The objectives of the museum are to interpret the impact of the Atlantic salmon on the Miramichi region, past, present and future; to educate people on the importance of the Atlantic salmon as a species and a game fish; and to promote conservation and good sportsmanship. Activities provided by the museum include river excursions ranging from a few hours to a few days, an established fly-fishing school and the teaching of canoeing fundamentals and guiding techniques.

Outside the museum, during the salmon season, the Atlantic salmon can be seen as they leap and play while returning home to spawn. The turbulent, brawling, fast-water pools of the Miramichi and its exciting game fish have been attracting the tourists here since the turn of the century. Indeed, the Atlantic salmon plays a vital role in the economy of the towns and villages of the Miramichi.

For the river folk and those who follow the migration of the Atlantic salmon, the Miramichi Atlantic Salmon Museum is a kind of shrine, a place to visit to discover more about this game fish and to celebrate its existence.

Miramichi Salmon Museum

Smith Forks salmon pool on the Little Southwest Miramichi.

ELEVEN
Casting for Slow Water

Whiskers

I once fished a salmon pool on the North Pole Stream (a tributary of the Little Southwest Miramichi) where the water was so fast a salmon couldn't catch the fly when presented on a normal swing. The hook was skipping and dancing across the water so that I had to stand on a rock in the centre of the river and fish it straight up and down. I have also fished stretches of the main Southwest Miramichi where the water was moving so slowly my line had very little swing, if any, and the fly had to be speeded up with hand movements to actually keep it from snagging the bottom. I've caught fish in both waters. These are extreme situations which I've used to make a point. Generally, the water flow will be somewhere between the two.

I have always found that fishing fast water is relatively easy in comparison to fishing slow water. It's a matter of casting at a 45-degree angle across the flow and letting the fly swing with the current, using a cast of a different length each time so that you are fishing clean and covering all the water. Fishing slow or dead water, on the other hand, is a different story, and few, if any, ever master the art. Many refuse to fish this kind of water, giving it up for a lost cause after many futile attempts, and leaving with the philoso-

Wayne Curtis plays a salmon on the Miramichi.

phy that fish won't hold in slow water for very long and, if they do lie in such places, they won't take a fly there because of the lack of oxygen. Both conclusions are false.

For those who have mastered the technique of slow-water angling, life on the river is fuller, more exciting and even less crowded, as they fish areas deemed unfishable above or below the traditional, crowded fast-water holding pools.

In all my years of angling, I have known few anglers who could present a fly in slow water so it would raise salmon with the same measure of success as the average angler could in fast water. Max Gillespie, the angling hall-of-famer from Blackville, was a slow-water expert. Jack Sullivan, who operated an outfit of camps in Blissfield for many years, was another. Jack could cast almost a hundred feet of line in all conditions and was an excellent slow-water fisherman.

Jack was a cousin of mine and I used to spend many hours sitting on the veranda of his cabin talking with him about fishing slow water. "You guys take the pool," Jack would say. "Crowd each other and beat the water, I'll fish down below the run." And he would go down the shore, perhaps a hundred yards or more, and start casting across the pond-like river with that long cast of his.

Casting for Slow Water

Once, at a sportsman's banquet in Doaktown (Conclave '86), I had a chance to chat with my two long-time mentors — Lee Wulff and Ted Williams — on the business of fly presentation. I had fished with these men individually and learned something from each about casting for slow water. They both agreed that presentation works over pattern at least 80 per cent of the time and that a superior presentation would compensate for a near opposite in pattern if one was restricted to a given hook. The same can be said of slow-water presentation versus fast-water. "If a fish can see the hook and it is presented properly, it will take almost any fly on any given day," Wulff said, adding, "but the fish has to be in a taking frame of mind."

The psych game was a big part of the Wulff philosophy on the matter. He felt that a salmon could be psyched into taking a fly and that if a hook hit the water and moved in the right direction at the right speed, a salmon would take it on impulse without having time to examine the pattern. I agree with this logic. We have to believe this.

Of course, there are some basic restrictions. If an angler is fishing slow water, he or she must fish slow-water flies; flies with long hackles and angled wings that breathe and swim in slow

Wayne Curtis on the Miramichi.

water if retrieved properly. The Ingalls Butterfly, the Rat-faced McDougall or hackled bugs such as the Green Machine are examples.

The big Southwest Miramichi, from the White and Gray Rapid regions upstream for 20 miles and beyond, is a big, slow-moving river. Much of the Cains River is the same. There are few fast-water holding pools that punctuate these reaches. There is certainly more water that is slow-moving than fast.

But in the slow water, there are submerged rocks which make "dents" on its smooth surface. These are the areas where salmon often lie. They also can be found in areas where no visible rock dents can be found. At first glance the water may appear unfishable. This is not always the case. The fish that lie in these areas will rise for the proper presentation.

This is the most exciting form of angling I know. If the fly is presented properly, the water will explode when the fish strikes.

Sometimes a fish can be seen following the hook for great distances. It is a strain on the nervous system to remain calm and scientific in such circumstances. In slow water, if the fish moves at all, it creates a commotion. Trout fishermen, who are used to

June salmon taken by the author.

setting the hook on sight, will always pull the fly away from a salmon.

I once fished with Art Flick, a famous American trout fisherman, who never once hooked a salmon in three days of fishing because of his impulse to set the hook before it was in the fish's mouth. This habit was from years of trout fishing and, as far as I know, he took it to his grave.

Growing up on the aforementioned stretch of the Miramichi River during the 1950s, I had to learn to fish slow water at an early age as a matter of necessity. By this time, many of the fast-water holding pools were already bought up by Americans and were crowded with anglers from away. When the Americans left, I fished their water and, even though it had become a part-time river for me, I will always be grateful to those men for sharing their salmon water with me, at least when they were not in camp. However, I did not attempt to fish the American water when they were here. It was impolite to do so unless you were invited. I fished the slow water between pools and I caught fish anyway, figuring out some of the presentations and discovering others by accident. For example, I hooked salmon on false casts more than once, which told me that these fish wanted the fly faster than the presentation I was using.

Where the water was really slow, I learned to cast almost straight across the water, slightly less than 90 degrees, so the line wouldn't have a curve in it and the fly would swim across and not streak down stream. It's important not to have any slack in the line, so that when the fly turns over and hits the water, it won't submerge, but will move quickly. More than that, when the good cast was made and the fly was still turning over in the air, I started to retrieve with short, smooth strokes, about the length of the rod grip. This gives the fly an immediate hit-and-move action. (The slow-water fly would take a swim stroke comparable to that of a water bug.) It is important to start the retrieve just before the fly hits.

This kept me very busy, but I had examined the presentation of anglers who were using a lazy 45-degree angle drift-type cast in the same slow water, and the fly was sinking almost a foot before the line straightened out and it started to move. Even though this is very unattractive to fish and it seldom works, in some cases a fish may have struck at the submerged fly and gone unnoticed with all the slack. When the water speed picked up, I slowed down the stroke and lessened the angle, which is not always as easy to judge as you might think.

I was once fishing a small holding area in the big river where the water was running out, off a point into the main flow. While the overall river was flowing straight away, the current in this area was running toward centre stream at nearly 30 degrees. I was fishing it at a 45-degree angle to the main stream, hooking fish but not landing them. My angle of presentation was wrong. But, after I read the water more carefully from below the pool (always go downstream, below the pool, to read the water) and realized the direction, I fished it at an 80-degree angle and took many fish.

TWELVE
At Liar's Rock

Blue Doctor

L iar's Rock is gone now, pushed away through the years by the ice jams, like so many lesser stones. Gone, too, are the many fishermen, outfitters and guides that gave the great rock its name. It was flat on top, like a bed, with a curved place to lie upon. In 1960 it was located at the centre of the long gravel beach at the Gray Rapids salmon pool on the Miramichi. Paul O'Hare had fishing waters along that stretch of river. He also owned and operated the Doctor's Island fishing camp in Blackville. As a teenager, I slept on the rock for at least two falls while working as his guide.

Paul resembled Groucho Marx and came from New York City during the late 1930s, fishing with his first wife in the Doaktown area. In 1941 they bought Doctor's Island from Alfred Underhill, who had acquired it from Archie Alcorn during Alcorn's bankruptcy. Underhill had been using the island as a cow pasture. (The original owner, however, was a Dr. Idare from New England, who gave the island its name before the turn of the century.) Paul and his wife hired Jim and Max Gillespie to cut logs and raft them down the river to the island where Frank Mountain, an expert cabin builder, built the main lodges at the top of the island, facing upstream.

Paul O'Hare

Paul smoked a straight-stemmed pipe, like Mark Trail, wore the plaid shirts and was a colourful figure in the Miramichi for years. He also owned a farm in Derby and, in the winter, ran a power saw sales and service shop with the assistance of Lloyd Sturgeon, one of his early guides. Lloyd had a motorcycle accident on April 9, 1951, and lost a leg. He never guided much after that, but was an excellent outboard motor and power saw mechanic.

Lloyd was the most knowledgeable fly-fisherman and the best caster I ever knew. After the accident, he taught my brother Winston and me how to cast a fly so it would light on the water and move as softly as a natural insect. We hooked our first salmon that summer of 1951, when I was eight. Lloyd also taught us the principles of the internal combustion engine: spark and explosion.

I was still underage when I started guiding for Paul in 1960. It was my first job away from home. I can still remember taking the Bible in my hand and being sworn in as a guide by Blackville game warden Al Lebans. Mr. Lebans chewed tobacco and added the words, "And are you positive you're eighteen?" to the oath. I was small but Mr. Lebans knew I had grown up around the sports.

Paul's foreman at the time was Max Vickers, and Max was very good to my brother Winston (Paul called him Win) and me. We joined Paul's team of guides along with Stafford and Norm Vickers (brothers to Max), Clarence Mountain and Gordon Munn. In Win's and my age group were Paul Gillespie and Alvin Harris.

Paul had many friends from the New York area who came to his camp regularly. Dr. John Losier, a dentist from Lynhurst, New Jersey, was one of them. Others were Sye Diamond, Guthery Cunningham, Colonel Pool, Aberly and Webb, Mack Mills and Danny O'Hare (Paul's brother). It was also here that Ted Williams of the Boston Red Sox came to fish.

I guided Dr. Losier for two falls and Win guided him for years after that. Dr. Loisier was an excellent angler and had fished with Lee Wulff on the Four Toe River in Labrador. He certainly didn't

Lloyd Sturgeon

need me to show him what to do, so my job was easy. He gave me a pack of Camel cigarettes each morning and, because he loved the Gray Rapid pool, we went there. I slept on the big rock while he fished.

Because Ted Williams was around, there was word that, possibly, Joe DiMaggio was also. Following this, there was always the rumour that Marilyn Monroe was in camp. I've since talked to an old-timer from the rapids who claimed to have guided the beautiful blonde. We were always looking for her to come out of a camp. If we saw a woman at some distance away on the river, for a moment it was Marilyn. To me, then, and still, any woman on the river is a beautiful sight. But Marilyn . . .

Anyway, all of this gave the whole operation a touch of romance. I have heard all my life that Marilyn Monroe fished here and I don't know for sure that she didn't . . . but she was here that fall, in spirit at least, and in the minds of us who watched for her.

I had a girlfriend in Blackville at the time; my first love. On those yellow and breezy September days, as I lay on the rock watching Dr. Loisier fish, I would think of her and of when I could get off to go and see her. I thought about Marilyn, too, and somehow, to me, the two women started to look alike. I loved both women equally and both were equally elusive.

Other celebrities rumoured to be fishing on the Miramichi were the actors Vince Edwards and, years later, Tom Selleck, who was reported to have bought out Ted Williams. The only real celebrities that I knew to fish here were, in fact, Ted Williams and his friend, boxer Jack Sharkie. Writer and film personality Lee Wulff fished here many times, as did musician Hoagie Carmichael in 1986. General James Doolittle and Stillman Rockefeller stayed at Wade's fishing camp in Howards in the 1950s.

One day when I was reclining on Liar's Rock and my mind was somewhere else, I heard a splash and shout, and rose to see the Doctor submerged, with only his head out of the water. I scampered into the cold river without waders and assisted him, coughing and sloshing, to shore. He had slipped on a rock and lost his balance. Afterwards, I waded in and retrieved his Thomas rod, glasses and drifting fly box. I can still recall drying Dr. Loisier's roll of grey 20-dollar bills, spreading them out around the circle of the fire. The following morning, when I arrived for work in long chest waders, Paul O'Hare and Dr. Loisier laughed for an hour. They always teased each other in such cases, reminding me of Abbot and Costello or the Marx Brothers.

But on the river Dr. Loisier was serious. He fished hard and he loved barbecued salmon. Each day before noon, my job was to gather hardwood and build a fire. From the camp we took only bread, tea and a grill. When he caught the first grilse of the morning he would ask me to cook it for lunch.

I would split the grilse up the belly and open it up flat like a snowshoe. Then I would lay it in the grill, flesh side down, over the hardwood coals. After 20 minutes, the leaves of the fish started to curl and it would be turned over and held, skin side to the coals, and scorched so the skin would come off in one piece to be thrown away. Then the backbone was removed (also attached), leaving only two pink slabs of salmon, which we ate with homemade bread and ten-minute-boiled river-water tea.

I will always be grateful to Dr. Loisier for teaching me how to cook a salmon on an open fire. He always emphasized how important it was to use hardwood and not charcoal or gas for cooking salmon, and to cook the fish flesh-side down as all the fat was in the skin and would drip through and keep the fish moist. I have cooked many salmon like this since, always with positive comment. Dr. Loisier became a friend of my family and we corresponded for many years afterwards. When Paul sold Doctor's Island some years later and moved to Montana, Loisier fished at the Wilson's camp in McNamee.

Even today, when I'm barbecuing a salmon at my cabin, the scent of the fish, the hardwood fire and the bush tea are reminders of those days when the cool September winds pushed up the river and the yellowing sun tried to warm me from those autumn blues at Liar's Rock.

It comes back to me, too, when I smell the smoke of an American cigarette (we didn't know that smoking was bad for us then, and considered it to be romantic), or hear a song by Peter, Paul and Mary or the Highwaymen. I think of how I could once glance across the river to watch the great Ted Williams, then a man in his forties, casting a long and perfect line. Below him would be Jack Sullivan, the flamboyant outfitter from Blissfield, with a guest or two. And there was always a blonde-haired beauty in the pool (she could have been with Ted or Jack), throwing a decent line. They'd shout to each other above the din of the water that bubbled around the waders. The constant upriver wind would toss the waves and put the whole scene in motion.

And the women, God bless them, from a distance, were always Marilyn Monroe.

Two grilse caught by Wayne Curtis in August.

THIRTEEN
Home Pool

Munro's Killer

*T*he team pulls the out-of-gear binder with ease, rattling as it goes to the flat, its driving wheel cutting slashes in the sod. Over at the edge of the oat field, Father kicks the machine into gear and the binder eats into the standing oats. The big grey wheel tilts the standing grain against the cutting blades. The side levers kick, throwing out the sheaves, and my younger brother, Danny, and I walk behind, picking them up by the twine and stooking them into wigwams. Afterwards, the blue jays flit among the stubbles. Danny gathers rocks from the highway and hunts them. He wants the feathers for a fly-hook.

After we have hauled in one load of oats and tiered the sheaves on a temporary scaffold above the barn floor, we go back to the flat for the second load. As I stick the pitchfork into the butt end of the sheaves and toss them into the hayrack, Father pushes them around, placing the ends out to make a neat, square load. He grumbles about the blackbirds eating some of the crop.

A white '57 station wagon with pink plates drives to the edge of the field. Its driver gets out and comes toward the wagon. He is overweight, grey haired and dressed in khaki.

*Authors Doug Underhill, Herb Curtis, David Adams Richards
and Wayne Curtis at the Oriole Lodge.*

"Now who the hell is that comin'?" Father says. "The high sheriff?"

"Is this the Moar farm?"

"Yessir!" Father answers without taking his eyes from his work.

"Would you be Mr. Moar?"

"Yessir!"

"My name is Sam Eagles. I'm from Connecticut. Someone said you folks might have a place to fish."

"Yessir!"

Eagles is about 60 years of age and puffs on a big cigar. He seems intimidated by Father.

"How's the fishing out front here?"

"The very best! But it depends what yer lookin' fer. Chubs? Eels?"

"Salmon."

"Yessir!"

"You mean there's salmon out front here?"

"Sure we have fishin', an' good fishin'. They'd be a salmon at the rock today, don't ya think, boys?"

"I saw one jump this morning," Danny says.

"Would you mind, Mr. Moar, if I took a cast or two?"

"Not likely, go ahead. But you'll need a guide." Father moves the sheaves about without looking now. "Danny, you go with 'em an' show 'em where ta fish."

"Beautiful, beautiful. Come along, Danny."

The American drives over to the riverbank and Danny helps him assemble his equipment. He puts together a long split-bamboo rod and gets a landing net from the car and gives it to Danny. He sets a tackle box on the ground and, with a small hand pump, begins to inflate a rubber raft.

"He's got 'nuff riggin' t'go after a whale," Father says. "He must have money. But we'll see if he's a tipper."

The September sun makes the stubbled fields and the trees along the river appear yellow. When the last of the oats are in the barn, Father gives a sheaf to each horse and I go to the river to watch the American fish. Danny has anchored the raft near the opposite shore and Mr. Eagles is casting into the eddy. Danny has anchored him in the wrong place on purpose, and when he sees me on the shore, he gestures that he has seen a fish at the submerged rock behind the raft. I watch for a while and, when the salmon breaks water, I go to the house to look for my fishing rod.

My rod has not been used since Danny fished with it in the spring. I find it standing among the raspberry bushes behind the outhouse. The reel contains very little line and the rod tip has been broken and repaired with electrical tape. I thread the line through its guides and pull down on the tip. It seems to bow evenly. But the rusted reel squeaks with grit and sand as I crank it and make casts in the yard. I go to Danny's room and find one of his blue jay flies. Knowing there is a salmon at the rock makes me feel that old pull to the river.

Father's board boat is moored on the rock beneath the overhanging grass, its paddle and pole afloat within. I bail, using the paddle like a shovel, and carefully set the oblong rock that we use for an anchor on the bow, coiling its chain nearby. Adrift, I pole toward centre-stream. The boat skims the water and waves lap against the hull. I brace myself in the stern, manoeuvring the old boat among the rocks. Soon the water is swift, frothing over the boulders and shallows of the gravel bar. I push the anchor overboard and its chain rattles over the gunwales, sounding like a machine gun in the hollow evening. The boat sways but holds fast; there is a tug from the anchor and I hunch on my knees to maintain the balance.

I cast the feathered fly-hook to where the water boils up behind Salmon Rock. The fly is followed by something deep that makes a swell as the line tightens. I give a reactive pull and the old rod bends.

"Fish on!"

"Wahoo! Heeya! Hold his head up!" Danny shouts.

The fish goes to the bottom and there is a scratchy screech from the reel as the rod maintains its even bow. The fish lies still for a few seconds and then swims downstream, making the reel hammer in its frame. Then it leaps above the water and shakes its head.

"Look! Look! Your brother's got one on! He's got a big fish on!" Mr. Eagles shouts. "Let's go and help him land it!"

I push to shore, paddling at intervals, keeping the line tight and the fish away from the boat. At one point, I hold the rod cork in my teeth and paddle. When the boat reaches shore, I scramble through the tall grass to regain some of the line, but can do little

Steven Curtis angling the Miramichi.

Wayne Curtis with CTV's Harvey Kirck as they prepare for a canoe trip down the Little Southwest Miramichi

better than hold my own in the rough going, until the fish swims into an eddy. Danny and Mr. Eagles follow.

The salmon raises to the surface so we can see its back. It's an old hookbill, the biggest I've ever seen. A kind of panic comes over me.

"How 'bout that!" the American says when the fish leaps out of the water, revealing its deep and brown speckled sides. "Look at the size of that fish!"

I sway the rod back and forth, trying to move the fish close. Then we walk downstream, Danny carrying the scoop-net.

"But did you boys actually see the size of that fish?"

"He's going upriver!" Danny shouts. "Let's run up the shore and get in some line!"

"It's okay! He's swung now with the current!"

The fish comes back into the eddy. We watch the yellow casting line as it disappears in the dark water, and strain for another possible glimpse. And then, in the repaired section of the rod, the tape gives away and the rod begins to buckle. As the fish moves deep and shakes his head, the outer half collapses and falls into the water, following the line toward the fish.

"The rod's breaking!" Mr. Eagles shouts. "Oh hell! Your rod's gone into the water!"

"You broke it!" I say to Danny.

"You knew it was broke!" he responds in the defensively unapologetic tone of guilty siblings everywhere.

I have only the rod's butt end and reel and, as I crank, I find I have no control. I try to pick up the slack as the fish swims toward us. At one point it is so close that Danny is reaching to scoop it. But when he has the net almost under the fish, it turns quickly and swims into the deep water, the rod's end trailing from its jaw.

"This should be his last run!"

"Danny, get ready with the scoop-net!" Mr. Eagles shouts. He has a camera on a strap around his neck and he takes pictures.

The fish comes into the shallows and, this time, Danny scoops it. We all help carry the salmon to shore.

Danny strikes the big fish on the head with a rock and it thrashes in the grass, and then lays quivering, its slimy flanks sticky with shore grass, sand and blood.

"That's remarkable!" Mr. Eagles says. "It must be 20 pounds!"

We take pictures of each other holding up the salmon.

"You boys need a decent fishing rod."

There is dew now, making our tracks visible as we cross the field toward the house. I have my hand in the salmon's gills and its tail is dragging. For the first time this year, the evening brings a damp, sour smell of autumn. We lay the fish on the floor of the outside kitchen and go into the house to get Father.

"Well, well, well," he says when he sees it. "Ya did well. Ya got one after all. And I didn't think there was a fish in the river . . ."

FOURTEEN
Ted Williams on Hook and Release

Grey Rat

While the majority of the salmon anglers fishing New Brunswick rivers are following the fishing laws and supporting government's attempts to save the Atlantic salmon by releasing the adult salmon, some anglers are still griping about having to put back the big fish," says Ted Williams, former baseball superstar with the Boston Red Sox. "Anglers should realize that replenishing salmon stocks now, by practising serious hook-and-release methods, is for their own best interest in the future. The survival of this major resource depends on it. These fish are now in the hands of the angler, literally. There is no one else we can blame if stocks decline."

Ted Williams was speaking from one of his salmon pools in a remote region of New Brunswick's Southwest Miramichi River. "I've been fly-fishing the Miramichi River almost continuously since the end of June," says Williams. "The fishing has been slow enough on most days. We're seeing all the fish, too. No fish are being taken commercially."

The former Triple Crown winner of the Boston Red Sox (in 1947, with 32 home runs, 114 runs batted in and a 343 batting average) has been fishing the Miramichi

Ted Williams ties up a salmon fly at his lodge on the Miramichi.
(Photo by Alex Fekeshazy)

River since before his retirement from baseball, back in 1960. He has always been an advocate of the hook-and-release theory. "I never kill a fish of any size anymore, and certainly not a female," he says. "It's a good feeling to release a salmon. I always feel better after I've done it and it's the best gift an angler can give to his or her favourite stream and to future anglers."

Williams claims that extreme care should be exercised in playing large salmon, and that they should be handled as little as possible before putting them back into the stream. "If it's done properly, all of the released fish will survive," he says. He considers it a great privilege to be able to fish for the Atlantic salmon, a privilege to catch them for the sport of it and release them, unharmed, back into the stream. He says, "It's the catching rather than the eating that is the most valuable. I like the old Lee Wulff line that says 'An Atlantic salmon is too valuable to be caught only once.'"

Williams emphasizes that New Brunswickers should be aware that the sports fishery could well be one of the province's best resources. Every effort should be made to see that this industry not only survives, but grows. He says, "A sports fish, of any kind, is worth its weight in gold to the economy."

Ted Williams on Hook and Release

Ted Williams leads a life that most sportsmen would consider an impossible dream. He spends his winters on the Gulf side of Islamorda in the Florida Keys. There he spends most of his time fishing for bonefish and tarpon, two game fish highly rated by Americans but fish that are rated by Williams as being nowhere near the value of the Atlantic salmon. "The Atlantic salmon is the best game fish in the world," says the great left-hander. "Nothing can touch it."

Williams noted that in the Florida Keys, sports fishing is now the major industry, and that any angler going there to fish for bonefish or tarpon could spend between $400 and $500 per day for guides, lodging and equipment. And they would have to release their catch. "Once in a while, a trophy-size bonefish or tarpon is saved for the taxidermist. But, for the most part, the fish are released. The guides make sure of that . . . it's their livelihood. With the fishing pressures being such as it is down there, if it wasn't for hook-and-release practises, these fish would have been wiped out years ago."

Williams believes that the business of salmon angling is expensive, but well worth the dollars for the enjoyment. He considers that each fish that he catches and releases costs him

The great Ted Williams fishing the Miramichi. (Photo by Alex Fekeshazy)

82

around $350 or $400. While the expense would be less for local people, it still circulates a lot of dollars into the economy. "I never complain about the expense," he says. "It's worth the money. Hopefully, someday, the fishing will be better, though."

Ted Williams first came to the Miramichi River back in 1955 when making a film. At that time, the river was rated as the world's best. After a short stint, he left, indifferent to the sport. Two years later, he returned and caught a 20-pound salmon and was hooked for life.

Before the season was over in 1958, Williams had purchased a mile-long stretch on the Miramichi River. Since then, the Miramichi has been his home for a third of every year. "Salmon stocks have declined since those days. But I don't think it's too late. If we, the anglers, are energetic and just a bit resourceful, we'll have a valuable resource in the years ahead," says Williams. Then he picks up his fly rod and begins throwing a line into the breeze.

FIFTEEN
On Paying Dues

Red Abbey

The large fish breathed freely as I held it underwater, facing into the current. It contained many thousand spawn and spawning time was not far off. When it started to jerk and jostle and was difficult to hold, I released my hands from it without hesitation and the fish scooted away in the direction of midstream.

We had had the pleasure of casting for this fish, raising it several times and eventually hooking it, plus the excitement of playing it on my light tackle. My son Steven had scooped it for me. Then, as we watched the female grilse swim away, we rejoiced at our decision to release it. We had made our contribution to the river with the gift of life. Surely this must be the best way to repay a stream for the many fish we had taken through the years. Releasing the grilse had made me feel like a true sportsman and hopefully fostered in my son a sense of responsibility toward the stream.

The greatest thrill in angling is releasing a catch after you have pursued, fought and won the battle fairly. The idea of paying back a stream for hours of pleasure spent is a contribution bigger than that of the average angler. It is the quickest and surest way to pay your dues to a river.

(Left) Lee Wulff and his wife Joan at a cabin on the Miramichi. Joan was a world casting champion. The couple fished around the world and ran a casting school on the Beaverkill River in New York State for many years.

(Right) Lee Wulff, the famous outdoor writer and filmmaker from New York, once sponsored the author in the Outdoor Writers Association of America (OWAA). Wulff was killed in a plane crash in 1991.

The Atlantic salmon is a prized game fish at any size. It is also an endangered species. Thus, the rewards for releasing are greater. A skilful angler does not have to prove his prowess to fellow anglers by displaying quantities of dead fish. He enjoys angling for the experience of being out of doors and the challenge of various strategies. Many fly-fishing elites have earned their reputations through their willingness to set free good fighters as payment for the experience.

Lee Wulff, a long-time outdoor writer, filmmaker and champion fly fisherman, began releasing Atlantic salmon over 50 years ago on Newfoundland's great Humber River and Portland Creek. Lee's belief was that the great fighters should be released to breed more great fighters, making river stocks better game catches for future anglers.

This was a long-term project. The Newfoundland rivers in the 1940s were teeming with Atlantic salmon. But even in those early days of salmon fly-fishing, Lee Wulff had the foresight to conserve the salmon and the stamina to withstand the ridicule from his fellow anglers. Today, a successful hook-and-release program is enjoyed by thousands of Americans near Lee's home in New York's Catskill Mountains.

Through these mountains flows the famous Beaverkill River. This is the most famous trout stream in the United States and the point of origin of American fly-fishing. Anglers from miles around drive to the Catskills on a regular basis to fly-cast for the famous brown trout which inhabit the stream. Considering the population in the Beaverkill area, with such cities as New York, New Haven and others nearby, it's amazing that, after so many years, they catch any fish at all. Yet because of their strictly enforced catch-and-release programs, they do enjoy fine catches. The population of anglers on the Beaverkill cannot be policed regularly and much is left to the anglers themselves and their devotion to protect their angling interests.

In 1980, the hook-and-release law was imposed on New Brunswick's rivers by the provincial government. This law, however, dealt only with large salmon in a move to protect brood-spawning stocks. But many so-called sportsmen were reluctant to comply and pried for loopholes in the policy. Prior to this law, only the angler devoted to saving the Atlantic salmon, such as sportsmen with the foresight of Lee Wulff, volunteered to release the great fish.

The Atlantic salmon is now on the list of endangered species. Many links in the chain have already been destroyed. To many anglers, the fate of these fish matters only in so far as they contribute to their reputations as fishermen. Our ability to save the Atlantic salmon from extinction could be a measure of our ability to save ourselves.

As sportsmen, our best contribution is to release a percentage of our catch. The reward will be there, down the road, if we remember to pay our dues to the river.

SIXTEEN
Black Salmon: A Special Challenge

Rose of New England
Courtesy of W.W. Doak & Sons Ltd.

J ust as the blackbird's first song of the season heralds the onset of spring and the promise of summer, the splash of a black salmon is music to the ears of of the angler who has been suffering a six-month bout of cabin fever. Indeed, a black salmon battling on the line can provide very welcome sport. It is a thrill not unlike hitting that first long drive down the centre of the fairway when your fellow club members are watching.

A black salmon angler must not follow the practices of a bright salmon angler when locating fish or even selecting the hook's presentation. As we've noted, bright salmon do not feed in fresh water. They are heading upstream to spawn, seeking fast water and gravel beds. They are fat, having fed heavily in the ocean, and seeking a mate. A black salmon, however, is a spent fish. Having spawned the previous November and lived under the ice during winter, it is now on its way downstream, where it is mostly carried by the water's flow, drifting with the current. Sometimes it rests in slack water, eddies or backwaters, often in bends where the water is deep. This fish is lean and hungry and must feed to survive.

Black salmon feed on small fish the such as smelts, chubs and suckers that often mill about in these waters. The large, buck-tail streamers used for angling black salmon match the hatch for these small fish. Popular patterns for black salmon include the Smelt, Golden Eagle, Mickey Finn, Black Ghost and the Rose Of New England.

Later in the spring when the water is brighter, the black salmon begin to jump and move more quickly to the sea, and they become harder to catch on a fly. Weighing more and no longer as hungry, and being in a moving frame of mind, they are less curious and will ignore almost any pattern or presentation. Like a bright fish, they will sometimes take the smaller salmon flies, cast in the same fashion as in summer. The river-wise will tell you that the late-spring black salmon are probably the best fighters of them all. By then they are lean and tough, having regained their former strength, and they use the heavy currents to their advantage.

In another sense, though, black salmon are easy prey. Much of the challenge is in the simple strategy of finding clean pockets of water and presenting bright enough streamers. Of course, at this time of the season you can get away with using larger and stronger tippets and a sloppy presentation with a large hook. In extremely dirty water, a sinking line may be advantageous. The river is much larger at this time of the year, so finding where the fish are is some of the fun. Eagerness to get afield in spring tends to hype up this outing.

The scientific approach in catching blacks is less sophisticated then with brights, but the spring spirit makes up the difference when it comes to internal rewards. Often black salmon stories are remembered for these reasons. When I look back at my own boyhood on the river, I recall mostly black salmon stories. My friends and family members used to make bets with me for the first fish landed in the spring. My brothers and I still do this.

One spring, after I had spent a few years living in the city, I came home in April to fish. The water was very high and dirty, but I stayed on the river all day in a severe snowstorm...and I caught fish. Because it was my first time out in so long, every fish I struck became more of a reward. Looking back, it is one of the few times I can recall spending a whole day salmon angling. Certainly it overshadows the many lacklustre August days when the fish aren't taking and the sport becomes simply routine.

SEVENTEEN
Striped Bass: New Sport on an Old River

Deer Hair Bass Bug

The striped bass is probably one of the most sought-after game fish in North America. They are fished along the coastlines of Canada and the United States, as well as in bays, mouths of rivers and into river estuaries. Dead water compounds throughout the continent have been stocked and thousands of spin-casting anglers pursue the rugged bass at tournaments and derbies everywhere. Indeed, as an all-round organized fishery, bass angling rates among the most popular.

Striped bass migrate along the Miramichi River system, too. From mid-May to mid-June, it is not uncommon to see a few dozen anglers fishing from boats or spin-casting from the shores in the estuary waters around Chatham and Newcastle and, to a larger extent, in the Tabusintac area of Miramichi Bay. The fish go up the river to the head of the tides at Quarryville.

These anglers fish from the wharfs, sometimes wading into the shallows, throwing long spin-casts toward centre stream and cranking the huge Repella Wablers or Skipping Bugs that attract bass. Occasionally they catch a big one, in the 20-pound range. But a good many of these bass are in the four to six-pound range, which is still a good fighting size.

Stripers are big bull fish, all head and teeth. They are not necessarily acrobatic, so don't expect heart-stopping leaps.

But they do have tremendous strength and are hard on tackle, taking many long and deep runs. A wire leader is recommended. Although they are basically night feeders, they will take through the day as well. They will take large bass poppers, massive streamers, up to an eight-inch floating plug, diving plugs, and heavy spoons as well as sand worms and sand eels. A skipping bug made of plastic is another effective lure. This resembles a crippled or escaping bait fish when jerked along the surface, and comes in a variety of colours: red and white, yellow and white, blue and white, all white and all yellow. The Repella Wabler is another small fish imitation, about six inches in length with trailing hooks and hooks stationed along its belly. It is retrieved slowly and near the bottom of the river. Blue is an important colour in this hook.

The method for fishing bass is simply throwing, retrieving and waiting for the strike. It is said that bass will take a number of coloured wablers on a given day, so detailed hook selection is sometimes overshadowed by a presentation that is neither scientific or delicate, but simply busy. In other words, choose quantity over quality.

Bass fishing arouses indifference in the majority of anglers that live on the Miramichi, or come to the region to fish. It is a relatively new sport here, even though the fish have been coming into the river for a good many years. I believe that at this point it is largely an experimental fishery, practised by an interested few. These bass fishers are salmon anglers by nature, adapting awkwardly to the spin-cast method for the sake of getting to the river a bit early. They spin-cast for the bass for that short part of the season between the runs of the more classic and sophisticated members of the trout family. Some prefer to fish the tides when they are on the ebb, while others fish the high tides.

Anglers come and go, replacing each other on the windswept and often drizzly wharfs, huddling in conversation. They roll cigarettes and treat each other. It's a pastime for the outdoorsman who seeks camaraderie. But there is not much romance in spin-casting for bass, even though this was a favourite sport of Ernest Hemingway. In the Miramichi it is looked upon by the scientific angling community as the mud race or demolition derby of fishing, as compared with the steeplechase or golf classic of the salmon and trout experience.

Bass do not fight the strong rapids to ascend the river above the head of the tide at Quarryville. They are mainly a bay and estuary fish.

Striped Bass: New Sport on an Old River

The author with a striped bass taken in the estuary of the Miramichi.

Although I can recall catching small bass well upstream when bait fishing for trout as a boy, I can also recall my father taking some larger bass from his gaspereau net and grumbling about their spiny horned fins ruining his net. Back then, I marvelled at their greenness and their incredible mouth of teeth.

While bass catches are said to be declining in other rivers since 1983, catches have remained stable for the few that have bothered to fish them in the Miramichi. PCB's and mercury contamination have been blamed for the decline in rivers like the St. John, although it is too early to tell if this is a real problem or merely a low spawning cycle. The U.S.-based Stripers Unlimited organization chose the Miramichi waters as a test site to compare the impact of pollution in the U.S. against the reproductive capabilities of our male striped bass.

As spin-casting is the only method for catching bass, and the Miramichi freshwater system enforces a law allowing fly-fishing only, the only waters open to this type of fishing are below the Quarryville bridge on the main Southwest and the Red Bank bridge at Sunny Corner on the Northwest estuary. The striped bass strike hard and run deep and fast, and hold well out into the deep, dark and otherwise silent waters of May.

EIGHTEEN
The Big Trout of the Miramichi

Green Drake

S
he's widely known and admired as one of the world's great salmon streams, but few are likely to give much recognition to the Miramichi as the home of tackle-busting trout. As a resident of the Miramichi Valley, however, I see the numbers of trout fishers steadily growing, as more and more anglers discover the big trout that run down to the sea and back again. I've been blessed and privileged to fly-fish the Miramichi and her tributaries for Atlantic salmon for most of my life. "Lucky" seems a woefully inadequate word to describe any fly-fisherman who can claim such a river as his home stream. In such circumstances, what remains a hobby for others becomes a way of life for the likes of me. But I too long regarded her as a salmon stream (albeit a superb one), and little more.

Speckled trout have always run in the Miramichi in large numbers in the month of June. Once upon a time they ran in schools that rivalled gaspereau and shad for sheer numbers. Because the river is scheduled, fly-fishing only is permitted above the tide. The challenge offered by these trout is thus enhanced, for they can be fussy, demanding the correct imitation, carefully presented. But in the river's estuary, where lures are permitted, many of these big speckles

Trout angling the Sabbies, a tributary of the Cains.

are taken by trolling or just spin-casting from shore with large spoons or spinners.

Last year, while working through a local salmon pool on Father's Day, I hooked something in midstream that acted like a small salmon. As the Butterfly touched the water and moved, on my retrieve, it was hit hard and line immediately peeled off the reel in a long run, but the fish never showed during the course of a 20-minute struggle. It was a five pound ten ounce brookie. I had fished her man and boy for over 30 years and had taken hundreds of trout from this hole, but this was by far the largest I had ever seen.

However, later at the general store, during the ceremonial weighing of the trophy, and chatting with the old-time woodsmen and river guides of the community, the shop keeper recalled numerous trout exceeding five pounds. One angler from Maine, Vincent Graves, remembered weighing a six pound five ounce fish in May of 1978. This was all news to me. Greatly encouraged, I hooked two more large trout that week in the same area and on the same fly. Needless to say, I have been heavily into Miramichi trout fishing ever since.

With the generally increasing interest and effort, the river has offered some fine trout fishing in recent years, with several fish in the seven pound range. However, the average boast-worthy sea-run speckled trout tends to be only two to three pounds. The cooler water near brooks or spring holes is where these fish are more likely to hold, but when the run is on they can be taken just about anywhere in the river.

The sea-run speckle trout, or brook trout, is native to the Miramichi. These fish move with the spring runoff downriver to the estuary, where they become fat from the rich feeding and bright as a consequence of making the physiological changes necessary to survive in salt water. In late May and June, they begin their return to the headwaters where they spawn, late in the fall — much like the Atlantic salmon, with the notable difference that they continue to feed. Like most salmonids, the male grows a hook or kype on its lower jaw as the spawning phase approaches and adopts an abnormally ferocious attitude, born of jealous territorialism. At this time, trout will strike fiercely at large streamers and frequently cannibalize their own eggs.

The Big Trout of the Miramichi

The all-time record speckled trout was a 14.5-pounder caught in Rabbit Rapids in Nipigon River, in northern Ontario, in 1915 by Dr. J.W. Cook of Fort William. All five of the weight-class world records listed since 1980 were taken in Canada, two from Quebec's Broadback River system and three from Labrador. All weighed more than eight pounds, and two were better than ten pounds. Not bad for a fish that, unlike its closely related cousins, arctic char and lake trout, rarely lives beyond five years.

While Miramichi brookies may not match those trophies, they are large by Maritime standards and are taken in moving water, which adds zest to the battle. While they are still running upriver, sea-run fish may strike at any fly you have in your box. We have taken many (often unintentionally) on salmon flies like the Butterfly or the Cossaboom. Dry flies were also snapped up, the Wulff series and Rat-faced McDougall being particularly productive.

It is claimed that brook trout will eat any living creature their mouths can accommodate, from insects and members of their own species to mice, snakes and snails. But after the water warms up and the fish have been in the river for a while, the game changes. At such times, you are more likely to encounter the fussy, frustrating trout we all know best, stubbornly locked into specific insect hatches and regularly rejecting poor fly-tying and sloppy presentations.

Trout taken on the Miramichi.

96

I have often matched the hatch for brookies with precisely the same care and attention to detail demanded by the shy, discriminating brown trout of the New England or British chalk streams. I have taken trout on late June evenings by carefully matching mayflies for size and colour, and I have sometimes lucked into a feeding frenzy induced by a green or a brown drake hatch.

During the latter part of June, tributaries like the Cains, Dungarvon or the Renous should be excellent for trout fishing. These smaller streams are generally ten degrees colder than the Miramichi during the dry months and speckled trout tend to seek temperatures below 68°F.

Lest I leave the wrong impression, it should be emphasized that many pan-size half-pounders will be encountered for every large trout fooled. Many local anglers freeze these in sacks of water and barbecue them on indoor fireplaces during winter.

The brook trout remains a highly sought-after game fish, the most popular in eastern Canada as a matter of fact, and it has brought about renewed interest in the Miramichi in that never-never-land between the black salmon fishing of spring and the bright salmon runs of summer.

NINETEEN
Grey Trout: Fighters from the Frigid Depths

Grey Wulff

The Indians called them *Namaychuk*. They are king-size trout that inhabit Canada's inland freshwater compounds. They have been known to grow to sizes of over of a hundred pounds and are strong battlers when tackled with hook and line. Better known as togue, grey trout, great lakes char or just lakers, they dwell in Canada's deepest and largest lakes, where they thrive in temperatures hovering just above freezing that are found at extreme depths. These fish are known to inhabit waters from the northernmost tip of the Yukon Territories and Alaska through the Atlantic provinces of New Brunswick and Nova Scotia. They are native fishes of these landlocked, underwater worlds and, since ancient times, masters of their kingdom.

In New Brunswick, the deepest and best producing compounds for togue are lakes such as: Long Lake, Chamcook Lake and Grand Lake. While many smaller lakes support fewer numbers, these waters probably hold the best populations throughout the Atlantic provinces. To the angler seeking high adventure the quest for this game fish can provide a great challenge. Careful strategists are rewarded with the thrill of a fierce battle and, probably, capture. The best time for angling the grey trout is in the early spring. Immediately after the ice melts away from the water surface, they are known to mill about in the then cool water, near the surface, before the temperature of the water begins to warm from the sun. Later they move to extreme depths, keeping below the warm-water level during the summer months, where they feed on white fish, insects and other trout fingerlings of their own species. During the early spring and late autumn, when they have moved to the shallows, they live on suckers and chubs, as well as insect hatches.

Angling for the grey trout is done from a large motorboat. The method used in early spring of trolling with long lines at a distance of about a jundred yards from shore is best. Large spoons about 18 inches long that flash on a light wire (shock tipped) with live bait near the hooks have proven the most productive. Other angling methods with depth finders and fish-finding devices are used in summer.

When the grey trout strikes, it quickly submerges to great depths, causing a battle royal for the angler. This fish will most often run vertically instead of horizontally. Unlike the Atlantic salmon, which is a leaper, a grey trout will never break water, but will always stay deeply submerged.

Some of the previously mentioned lakes in Atlantic Canada have been restocked. For instance, officials have released 3,400 prime brood-stock fingerlings into New Brunswick's Long Lake. A restriction has been made that any grey trout caught that are under 14 inches must be released.

The largest known grey trout captured in North America was taken in a gill net in Lake Athabasca, Saskatchewan, on August 8, 1961, by Mr. Arton Flett. It weighed 102 pounds and was 49 inches in total length. The angling record for North America is 63 pounds 2 ounces for a trout caught in Lake Superior in 1952. In most inland lakes, however, the average catch is less than ten pounds. With the grey trout's reproduction rate, great angling is expected in Long Lake in the years ahead.

The grey trout's spawning habits are similar to that of the Atlantic salmon. They whisk their spawning beds clean with their tails before the progeny is deposited. They spawn in areas of boulders where the water is shallow. Threats to the unhatched spawn may exist in some large lakes that support hydro plants, where lake depths can vary by six or eight feet. The eggs also become a prime food supply for the yellow perch and other coarse fish that thrive in this part of the lake.

The number of eggs deposited depends on the size of the female but ranges between 400 and 1,200 eggs per pound of female. Officials claim that a 32-inch female may deposit up to 18,000 eggs. When the eggs hatch in February or March, they grow fairly quickly and can reach lengths of 18 - 20 inches in three or four years.

The lakes of Atlantic Canada that the grey trout inhabit appear to be untouched by airborne pollution, acid rain or PCB's. The fish here remain edible. Many northern Ontario lakes have been ruined by the deadly acids, and the grey trout have vanished from their waters completely.

TWENTY
Fishing Shad

General Practitoner

I have never deliberately gone fishing for shad (or any coarse fish), but, to my disappointment, I have caught a good many by accident while angling for bright salmon in June. So, they will take a fly-hook. However, I am told that an increasing number of salmon and trout fishermen have now taken up shad angling as a means of recreation during the two or three weeks they are in the river.

As pressures grow on the salmon and trout fishery, the pools become crowded and over-fished. But during the shad runs in late May and early June, there are few people on the river. And, of course, while these fish are white and extremely bony, they can be very tasty when cooked properly.

Shad come into the river behind the smelt and gaspereau runs, slightly ahead of, or with, the first runs of bright salmon. They number in the millions, and they play and splash, scooting around in slow-water areas, sometimes spooking and upsetting the more sophisticated salmon. They are a nuisance to early salmon anglers, too (once I saw an American cast for hours over an area where a shad had splashed—thinking it was a salmon, I suppose). While shad stocks have declined during the 1970s and 1980s, they are now returning in numbers that are approaching old-time levels.

Fishing Shad

When I was growing up on the Miramichi in the 1950s, it was common to stand on the shore and count 50 shad, stacked like fish in an aquarium, in the eddy near home. For excitement we jigged them with trout hooks, but we landed very few, as they capered and ran at speeds faster than a salmon's. Their fight was short-lived and they never jumped, but splashed the surface with their tails like so many beaver.

There was an overpopulation of shad back then and a good many died before returning to the sea. Their decayed bodies drifted along and circled in the eddies and got caught up in the bushes. Their odour mixed with that of lilac and cherry blossom, giving the river a sweet-sour smell. We had very little respect for shad back then.

Today, shad are once again ascending the main river as far as Boiestown and beyond, and in lesser numbers in large tributaries such as the Northwest, the Little Southwest and the Cains. With the abundance of people now using our river, angling for shad has become a fishery of its own. This, of course, happened to other rivers long ago (the Connecticut and its tributaries and other American rivers, and, to a lesser extent, rivers along the south shore of Nova Scotia). As salmon stocks declined, more attention was given to shad, so that they became a kind of poor man's salmon.

Jerry Doak, owner of the W.W. Doak & Sons tackle shop in Doaktown, describes the basic shad fly pattern as follows: a Redhead, sometimes with plastic eyes, a silver body with a red or sometimes yellow tail sprig of turf, a white wing of deer, goat or polar bear hair with a bit of crystal flash mixed in and tied on a number 6, down-eyed double hook. Doak adds that most fly-fishers prefer using the double hook for shad, which is considered unsportsmanlike when salmon angling. This can be justified as shad have a very bony mouth, and a great number are never landed anyway. A sinking fly-line cast upriver and mended (as in steelhead fishing) allows it to sink and drift down.

So, the fish that we once considered a nuisance, like in the U.S. and Nova Scotia, has become a popular game fish here. As my father used to say, "It's shad, but true."

TWENTY-ONE
That Ol' Cains

Copper Killer
Courtesy of W.W. Doak & Sons Ltd.

"**L**ord knows," my father would say, "that ol' Cains was always the very best of fishin' we had in the late season when the run was on."

When I was in grade six, I loved the river and hated school. But this was Saturday and I was here with Father on the Cains, free for the whole long Thanksgiving weekend. I was Nick Adams, Huckleberry Finn and Tom Brown combined; like Adams, I carried a good luck charm in the form of a rabbit's left front paw. Father was an outfitter on the main stem Miramichi in those days and he would often bring his guests to the Cains during October, when the season was closed to angling on the main river.

On my days away from school I was a go-fer, helping with the sports. But on this Saturday, Father had brought me here for company while he hunted the abandoned fields and ridges for the winter's supply of deer meat. By this time, I had spent many weekend hours exploring the friendly groves of hemlock, spooking woodcock along the river's elm tree intervals and stalking grouse in the black alder swamps near the back meadows. This day, we had pitched our tent in a clearing near the river and Father had gone for a walk with the gun. I stayed at camp, bonfire lazy.

The double hook is seldom used today because of the hook-and-release laws.
(Photo by Alex Fekeshazy)

The mid-morning silence was broken by the thrashing and splashing sounds that came from the river, and I sneaked to the bank to witness what I thought must be a moose wading in the shallows. Instead, I saw a large black bear sitting on its haunches on the beach, eating a large salmon. The bear spotted me and ran into the trees, the fish swaying in its jaws. I never saw the bear again, although I watched the rest of the day, hoping to catch it fishing. Perhaps it just moved upstream a mile or so away from our camp — I don't know.

But I saw plenty of salmon showing: large fish capering and splashing as they headed upstream over the shallows. Half-exposed, they wriggled in the run, striving for traction by fanning their tails and sending sprays of miniature rainbows against the breeze. Throughout the day, dozens of huge salmon schooled past me in the same fashion. Later in the fall we learned that game wardens had arrested a salmon poacher in that area. He had been shooting the spawning fish with a large calibre rifle as they went over the bar.

That night in our tent, the smell of kerosene and the stench of musty canvas was almost choking, but it didn't bother Father as he sipped his brandy and talked of old experiences on the river and of guests from days gone by. Even today, when Father talks of the Cains, he speaks of her personified, as he would of an old friend — positive and a little defensive.

"It was always a river to canoe," said Father. "The sports wanted to 'run her down.'" The boats would have been brought in on the old Portage Road with a team of horses and the double truck wagon. They always launched their canoes at a place we now call the Moores. The expedition would tent along the shore on the way downstream. Sometimes they would set up camp at Salmon Brook or at the Old Buttermilk Brook landings and sometimes at Uncle Andy Porter's field.

I make my annual pilgrimage to the Cains River each autumn, fishing the old established salmon water; pools with community names like Church Pool, Schoolhouse Pool and the Oxbow. Once on the river, I feel overtaken by the old, kindred spirits. For generations my family has been coming here and enjoying this river region during autumn so when I arrive, vignettes of my own boyhood appear like tiny portraits to the inner eye. My mind's eye fixes on the vivid details of an idyllic adolescence — the magic of my memories of youth enhanced, I suppose, by the distance in time.

Like the mighty Miramichi itself, the Cains is more than just a geographical location: it's a state of mind. A scenic little river, once

The Cains River hookbill. (Photo by Alex Fekeshazy)

105

renowned for its fall salmon, the Cains flows through the northeastern New Brunswick hinterland, meeting the Miramichi some 20 miles above Tides Head. Winding bends of white gravel beaches and hardwood shoreline summits, combined with a gentle flow, have always lured canoeists to its shores. In the headwaters that drain into the feeders, the water is tinted amber from the barrens, and the salmon are speckled and orange-bellied. While the once spectacular runs of fall salmon have fallen to low levels in recent years, a strict management regime has brought about the beginnings of a recovery. Potentially, this little river could become the best fall salmon river in North America; moreover, unlike the privately owned Miramichi, the Cains is 90 per cent open water.

Grandfather used to have a lumbering operation here, and logs were skidded along the steep hill overlooking the river, to be stream-driven in the spring. ("Your great uncle cooked for the crew, and he was a makeshift fiddler.") I can almost hear the old echoing in the crisp air. ("Big men sitting around lumber camps in high hob-nailed boots, plaid shirts and breeches — symbolic of the rivermen in the old days.") I feel the same pull of nature running through my ancestors, the old river and me.

On this day, I have parked my station wagon at a spot that overlooks the Moores. This is a long, choppy bend of salmon holding water. It is a brilliant Saturday morning in October. My son Jeff is behind me in the pool. He is home from university for the Thanksgiving weekend. He stays at a distance, but within talking range. I notice him taking a jaunt along the beach, maybe searching for an ancient arrowhead or a woodcock covey. I see myself in him, and he is perhaps discovering a part of himself he hadn't known.

At dawn, I had raised a salmon at the top of the run, but no strategy, presentation or fly pattern that I could offer would bring the fish to rise again. A sharp autumn breeze with a ghost of winter is fanning the water's surface, making it sparkle silver in the late morning sunlight. I continue to work my casts at angles across the water, watching for another possible rise and enjoying the background sounds of nature. Above the din of the bubbling river I hear the screeching of a Canada jay against the forest wall in the low meadow hawthorns. In the small rapids below me, a salmon is leaping above the water as it moves upstream.

Suddenly, almost in slow motion, a salmon tips itself on the surface in the area of my fly. The great fish leaves a wake that holds together like a ring drifting away in the current. "A likely taker," I think. A split second passes and I feel a gentle pull from below the surface. My bamboo rod bends double as I pull up to set the hook. The fish stays still on the bottom, as yet oblivious to being hooked, giving me time to wade onto the beach.

My line cuts through the water, taut and alive, indicating a fragile but positive contact with the Royal Coachman in the fish's mouth. We are as one: fish, line, fingertips, heart. The fish moves slowly over the washed gravel, rattling my nerves and making my heart a pounding bass drum that smothers the sounds of everything else on the river. There is a dark feeling of unease as the rod bounces from the savage shaking of the salmon's head. The fish turns fast with the current, causing an angry screech from the reel.

The salmon runs downstream and, in the classic high leap that symbolizes the fighting Atlantic salmon, shows silver and gold against the dark green shoreline. There is another head-shake and the line goes slack: the fish is free. For a brief moment I feel empty inside.

We go back to the top of the run and start down it again, casting all the different angles, all the flies, waiting for the salmon to strike. We fish and chat now, above the sound of the water, shooting holes through the breeze with each cast, as fishermen on the river have done for generations.

We share the old river and wait for the sudden, pleasant interruption of a taking fish.

TWENTY-TWO
A Fish Tale

Rat-faced McDougal

*T*he sky grew lighter. I paced the veranda floor of my log cabin while waiting for my brother Win. He was supposed to have picked me up at daybreak to begin our fishing trip on the lower reaches of the Cains River.

For months we had discussed this trip and, on this cool September morning, I was bubbling with anticipation. We would drive the ten miles up to Shinniks Corner, put in the canoe, and run down the Cains to its mouth. From there, we would continue back down the main Southwest Miramichi to my cabin — about 15 miles of river in all.

The fog was dense on the Miramichi that morning. I could hear the occasional splash of a jumping fish and the echo of a paddle bumping against a canvas canoe as someone went out into the home pool. The only other sound was the distant clatter and bang of an early-morning pulp truck on the stony road that led to the Cains.

Either I am over-anxious or he has over-slept, I said to myself as I paced like an expectant father. Finally, Win's station wagon, with canoe on top and lights beaming through the fog, bobbed across the elm tree interval to the Oriole camp, and we were soon on our way.

I'd been fishing the Miramichi since the days of the log drives, but I had never run the Cains. I had always heard the

Northwest Miramichi. (Photo by Guy Aube)

older guides, including Win, talking about the Cains River runs. Many local fishermen take this trip in the autumn, since this is a late river. I had seen as many as a dozen canoes drift by our camp in a single Sunday evening in September.

As we readied our canoe at Doug Cashin's shore, a large hookbill salmon broke water in slow motion. Although we were anxious to get moving, Win insisted on trying this salmon with a cast. As I stood in the canoe, he made a short cast downstream, checking for distance. Then he laid the Sunday punch right on the money, as they say.

With foam still heavy on the water from the September dew, the old hookbill bobbed his head out and seized Win's Copper Killer. A good 17 pounds, he jumped twice. I was running with the net when the hook flew out on a head shake. We were left standing disillusioned in the tall grass.

It was about eight o'clock when we finally pushed off.

About 90 per cent of the Cains is open water, so we didn't have to worry about taking someone's resting fish. There are a few private pools, though, and these we edged through, paddling close to shore so as not to disturb anything.

On many bends the river is narrow and fast. We tried the most likely spots, pools with names like Oxbow and Whirlpool. By nine-thirty I had a ten-pounder. This one I hooked on a Silver Grey in a narrow channel at the foot of an island.

After a late breakfast of bacon and eggs cooked over a hardwood fire, some refreshments to ward off the chill and a poem or two from the Robert Service book, we moodily paddled through the afternoon. Having made good time early, we did more fishing as the day wore on. We tried a few casts over the Pigeon Ledge pool, Salmon Brook, Buttermilk Brook and the Long Hole Rapids, with only the occasional rise.

Eventually the sun began to sink behind the hills, leaving the river shaded and making it seem closer to evening than it really was. We decided we would have lunch at the Slide pool. While I was preparing the chili, Win hooked a small salmon and beached it after a short struggle.

From this point down, the water was fast. We passed through the Hydro pool, Brophy pool and Hell's Gate Rapids. Soon we were looking at the church steeple at Howards, at the mouth of the Cains.

Angler playing a salmon on the Northwest Miramichi. (Photo by Guy Aube)

A Fish Tale

Another half hour and we were back at the home pool. With only about 20 minutes of fishing time left, we decided to fish out the remaining daylight in this vacant piece of water.

I chose to wade on the north side, as I always do. Win pushed the canoe across to within about 40 feet of the opposite shore and dropped the anchor. I cast a lazy Rat-faced McDougal near Poppa's Rock in the centre of the pool, where the water boiled. When the dry fly swung in the boil, a 14-pound hen fish came up, took my fly and headed across the river, burning my fingers on the line.

As she headed straight toward Win's canoe I remembered the anchor rope and yelled, "Fish on!" The salmon was still gathering speed and I could feel her coming toward the surface, as though to jump. Sure enough, about two feet this side of the canoe, the salmon leaped, splashing water on Win and landing on its belly in the middle of the canoe. Win had turned around to pull the anchor, but quickly fell on the thrashing fish and wrestled it down. He now had three salmon in the canoe, my limit of two fish and his one.

He removed my hook from the fish and dropped the fly over the side. As I reeled the skipping Rat-face, which was swinging deeper in the pool, another fish rolled and grabbed it. Since I already had my limit of two for the day, I tried my best to lose this one, a grilse. With my rod held straight out in front of me, and giving him slack, I shook the rod when he jumped. But no go, the fish stayed on.

Quickly I reached down and tailed him and, without taking the grilse from the water, released the fly. The fish swam away.

I sat down on the shore to have a smoke and to relive the sudden events. Father came down to check the canoes. He looked around the shore and bar for a minute, saw nothing and turned to me.

"No fish tonight, Wayne," he said. "Water's too high."

TWENTY-THREE
The Great Northwest

Cosseboom Special

*I*t was late morning when veteran river guide Ralph Mullin and I loaded our fishing tackle into the canoe and pushed off from Miners Bridge. We were set to run "The Loop," a fertile, fast-flowing stretch of water on the Northwest Miramichi River.

The river was at peak flow but no longer rising. Heavy showers during the night had left the sky clear, and the breeze, crisp with the freshness of June, carried a sweet incense of blossoming wild cherry and lilac. The only sounds were from the river: a din of bubbling and gurgling from the fast-flowing water, and the lapping against the hull. A family of mergansers pushed downstream before us, half swimming, half flying, always scuffling out of view beyond the next bend.

Mullin, tall with greying hair and a broad smile, sported a hard-shell safari hat. Bracing himself in the stern, he poled with confidence, gently manoeuvring his self-made canoe among the boulders. Nearly half a century as a fishing guide and a canoeist on the river has made finding the channels almost second nature to him. He steered around shallow waters and held our canoe back in churning rapids to avoid too much speed among jagged rocks. Stabbing at the river bottom with the pole, at times he forced the craft to a complete standstill.

The Loop, so called because it makes a huge semi-circle about ten miles long between two bridges, is the most accessible route for canoeist starting at Miners bridge on the Chaplin Island Road (Hwy. 430) and ending at the Wayerton bridge further down the highway. It is a short day's canoe trip on fast-flowing water.

Most of the water appeared to be worth fishing. On that day, though, many of the salmon were challenging the current, and moving upstream, launching themselves into the air in great, long leaps that appeared to be almost in slow motion.

At the head of a huge rock within a half mile of the launching area, Ralph hooked a fine 12-pound salmon. After an exciting display of reel-singing jumps and a good deal of scrambling by Mullin and me, it was finally netted and tagged. My companion, I discovered, could hold the canoe with one hand on the pole and battle a salmon with his free arm.

By one o'clock in the afternoon we had two 12-pounders in the boat. The other one had risen to my short cast as Mullin had held the canoe at the top of a rapids and I drop-fished from the bow, casting a streamer into the run. Having landed two salmon before entering the established pools, it became obvious that we could easily catch our limit well before completing The Loop.

I soon discovered some of the noted salmon pools within the bridge-to-bridge run; pools waiting to be tested, accessible only by canoe. We casted over the Ledge pool, Wilson pool, Salmon hole and Cedar pool, before completing our quota with two grilse at the Dennis pool, ending a day on the river which remains forever etched in my memory.

While these pools will generally produce salmon on any given day if fished properly, it is the larger holding pools downstream such as Wildcat, the Turnip Patch and Hawthorne, which have become shrines of fly-fishing throughout the Maritimes and the northeastern United States.

The Northwest Miramichi has earned a great reputation among anglers such as Mullin who have long fished here successfully. For many years anglers have boasted of its fine production, its location, its consistency and its accessibility. Some proclaim it to be the best Atlantic salmon river in the world, as it is perhaps the most productive tributary of the mighty Miramichi system.

The Northwest tumbles through the black spruce hills of northeastern New Brunswick, its upper reaches supplying a rod-per-day fishery with the finest Crown Reserve stretches in the province. Farther downstream, its open-water stretches descend for many miles, brawling over ledges and fields of giant boulders, dashing through deep-shaded bends of the extreme wilderness to the shaded elm tree islands and abandoned farmlands of the old settlements.

Here in the abandoned farmlands, the holding pools support rotations of successful sport-fishers on most summer days. As the river bends seaward, tributaries emerge. Rivers such as the Sevogle and the Little Southwest make their entrance before the Northwest flattens into a broad, slow water that glides past township and Indian village to form a common estuary with the main stem at the town of Newcastle.

In town, during early summer, the Northwest Miramichi becomes a topic of conversation for the many anglers and canoeists who gather to fly-fish for the Miramichi salmon. Here, residents and non-residents alike gather on street corners and tackle shops, swapping yarns of the river. Through such river people, Newcastle has become known as the Atlantic salmon centre.

Seated upon the flats of the estuary backwater, the town of Newcastle figures strongly in the history of this river. Here the awning-drooped, false-fronted stores and quaint gift shops join around the town square. The church spires that gleam above the ancient elms, together with the town's Victorian houses, serve as reminders of the history of a town always connected with the Atlantic salmon.

The squires and land dealers who once lived in the town granted land along the river to the settlers for the promise of working the land and establishing family farms; for the settlers, the river was the only means of communication. To encourage new comers, promises were made of caribou, moose ... and plenty of salmon.

The Northwest is the Miramichi's earliest producing tributary. During its great June salmon runs, many local anglers canoe its waters daily — the only way to learn the ways of the river. Increasing numbers of anglers float its waters each season, in appreciation of some of the world's best salmon water. But for the professional fly-fisher, canoeist and river guide (such as Ralph Mullin), each trip is a pilgrimage.

TWENTY-FOUR
The Delightful Dungarvon

Usk Grub

I have fished the Dungarvon River many times in the months of July and August and have taken salmon and grilse in difficult conditions with various kinds of fly combinations and strategies. I have also fished here in June with expectations of those early-run large salmon that challenge the turbulence of the little river. I've taken trout, at this time, in the half-pound to one-pound class, and many smaller. But I'm not a trout fisherman at heart, so when I drive the stony road to Dungarvon during the month of June, I am in search of early-run Atlantic salmon.

The Dungarvon is a small, fast-flowing river that sweeps through the rolling hills of eastern New Brunswick and finds its way into the Miramichi via the Renous. This river, though quite consistent for its size, is primarily an early-run salmon river and, if it were anywhere else in North America, it would get a lot more attention. Like most streams that are easy to reach, it would be over-fished. Overshadowed by the main river, the Miramichi, it is sometimes overlooked, but this little tributary is probably the best little salmon river in New Brunswick.

There have been many poems and ballads written about the Dungarvon. The most famous of these is *The Dungarvon Whooper*, a poem written by Michael Whelan, a poet from

A pool on the Dungarvon. (Photo by Doug Underhill)

Renous. The poem is a legend about a lumber camp murder that had ghosts whooping and yelling about the burial spot in the middle stretches of the river. Once on the river, you can understand how some people who are poetically inclined could get inspired to such a degree that they would quote lines of poetry and have visions of lumberjacks working the log drives.

I listened to my late grandfather tell fireside stories about the Dungarvon for many years. He talked of the famous salmon hole where he and poet Joe Smith, in a dugout canoe, speared a wagonload of fall-run salmon one rainy night many years ago, to supply a lumber camp with fish for the winter.

One thing I have always heard old guides say is that there is more water in a small fast-flowing river like the Dungarvon than there appears to be — more water than in some other rivers around that are larger looking but slow moving. The Dungarvon is fed mainly by springs, which keeps it very cold in low-water conditions.

Grandfather told us of pools like Red Pine Landing where, while driving logs in late April, the cook for the crew caught a bright salmon. It was in the evening when he left the cook scow and somehow caught the salmon near the end of a log jam. What the cook on that drive used for tackle was never discussed. He cleaned the shiny fish and quickly buried it in the coolness of a nearby snowbank, only to have it eaten up in the still of the night by hungry bears.

Often now, when fishing there, I think of Grandfather with regret that, perhaps, those stories are gone forever.

One year, while fishing the Dungarvon on the 14th of May, I hooked a bright salmon that had me talking to myself for days. It was at the Highway Bridge pool, about ten miles (by road) up from the village of Blackville. My family was setting up a picnic on the gravel beach. Our old setter, Shanesworth III, was wading recklessly in the shallows at the top of the pool, much to my displeasure. I was fly-fishing casually down through the pool, using a small version of a black salmon streamer called the Mickey Finn. Trout were hitting it occasionally, but they were just pan-size brookies. Casting at random as I walked the beach, I happened to cover a rock where a small boil joined on the far side. When my fly swung through the boil, a fish rolled deep, but let the fly pass. At first I thought I had rolled a large trout, but after a few more casts I rolled the fish again. This time, it was a good clear water-breaking roll and I knew it was a salmon. I thought it could be a black salmon, since these fish sometimes stay in the river until late spring, after a big year (I once caught a black salmon in the Miramichi River on the 9th of June).

I rested the fish for a few minutes and nervously threw the Mickey Finn over the rock again. Sure enough, the water exploded and the huge bright salmon seized the fly with great authority and the battle was on.

If there is one part of this game that excites me most, it is hooking a bright salmon when they are rolling fat, fresh in from Greenland and just a bit hyperactive. Of course, this day, I didn't bother to bring along a scoop-net!

I played the fish for a good 15 minutes, through water-churning leaps and bounds, and I believe that if I had had a net, I could have scooped it up on at least two occasions. Going downstream (my kids holding the dog) I was trying to beach it when the hook worked loose and fell out on a roll-over-nose turn. I spent the rest of the day cursing those fingerling trout. We had lunch on the gravel bar and drove slowly back to our camp on the Miramichi, visions of that leaper of the Dungarvon fresh in our memory.

Upon my return to the Dungarvon River in the week that followed, my dad, George Hennessy (a friend of ours from a neighbouring cabin) and myself, hooked and landed three salmon in three different pools there. Dad took one in the 18-pound range the following evening and George a 16-pounder the morning after. Both these fish were taken on salmon flies called the Black Ghost—a black-bodied fly with silver wrapping and white wing.

My fish however, was taken on the same Mickey Finn and was considerably smaller; somehow, an anticlimax. Reluctantly, I was on my way to a four-fish season on the delightful Dungarvon.

Doug Underhill angling on the Renous.

TWENTY-FIVE
On Past Favours

Garry

The community was one of scattered wilderness farms, all of which bordered the river. Each one was apart from the other and had its own personality, the spirit of its owner. These farms were united as a community largely through bonds of respect for the other man's property and his welfare. In a transaction with a neighbour, the nod of a head was as good as a signature. Philosophies were exchanged over line fences at haying time. Imaginations were nourished by loneliness and each one's strongest characteristics were developed from exposure to themselves alone. Indeed, there were characters here in Moores Siding, and as a youngster I knew them all.

There was old Tom Wills who walked at night, talking to himself in a variety of tones and answering in imaginative voices, so that, if you didn't know him and you heard him coming in the dark, you'd swear it was a crowd of men. Then there was old Charlie Eighton from the next farm. Chuck was a confirmed salmon poacher. Folks said it wasn't so much that Old Man Eighton wanted the fish he caught, but that he got his kicks from the risk of being caught sweeping a pool. For excitement he would poach in broad daylight. It was in his blood.

The fish wardens in those days were Ed Black and Raymond Mills. Old Ed was obsessed with his responsibility. "I'm sworn to protect the Atlantic salmon," he would say. "A dangerous species." He would help keep the balance in nature by saving the salmon link in life's chain, thus preserving mankind from extinction. It was said that Ed and Raymond would chase a poacher through the gates of hell. All of us at Moores Siding had great respect for the wardens.

In the mid-1950s, the fish wardens travelled the river by canoe and they became accustomed to long river runs of two or three days at a time; not an easy life. It was common to see them pitch a tent on the riverbank near our farm and spend the night there. I can recall watching from the hilltop and catching the fragrance of fish fillets sizzling on their campfire, which snapped by the lee side of a canoe propped among the bushes. While Ray and Ed were from some 30 miles up the river, they soon became close friends of my father's, as they sometimes used our interval for a tenting area.

One autumn evening, after the salmon angling season was closed for the year, the wardens made camp on the flats as they always did — only this night, Father invited the two men to our farmhouse to share the evening meal with the family. Ed and Ray were treated with heels of rum and the last drop of Scotch whisky in 20 miles. Voices loudened as they talked and laughed with Father, all cronies now in the old dining room.

Ed was telling Father of giving chase to an awkward poacher that same afternoon. "Yes," said Ed. "He was drifting with a long net, right through the salmon hole, just up around the bend from here . . . and in day-time! The gall of it!" He went on to tell Father of the man scrambling to get away, running up the steep riverbank with the wet salmon net dragging in the grass, a couple of large salmon becoming entangled. "He ran into a poplar treetop, left there by beaver," Ed continued. "His net caught up in the branches and he had to leave it with a large salmon meshed, dead. But the son-of-a-whore got away with one, or maybe two, large salmon."

He told us the poacher threw rocks from the hilltop, trying to hit them while they were untangling the net from the tree branches and putting it into their canoe. Ed then proceeded to lecture all of us on the dreadful condition of the resource, the amount of poaching that was going on and the trash that hung around the river in these parts, and how poaching would affect us all someday.

Novelist David Adams Richards on the Renous River. (Photo by Doug Underhill)

There was a rap on the kitchen door and, without waiting for an answer, Charlie Eighton entered the house. Charlie was in a fresh change of clothes, sporting his new plaid Mackinaw and his best felt dress hat. Under his arm he was carrying a large salmon of about 20 pounds. He was probably repaying Father for a past favour, or maybe it was just a gift to a loyal neighbour. In any case, the salmon was completely wrapped in newspapers, from its head to beyond its tail. Charlie walked up to the dining room table where the men were grouped, the fish tucked neatly under his arm.

When he saw the two uniformed wardens sitting at the table, he said, "Here, Jack. Here's the rifle I borrowed from you last week."

He passed the long salmon nervously across the table to Father.

"Indeed!" said Father, and at once took the newspaper-wrapped fish across the dining room and stood it in the corner. Then he came back to the table and went on with his evening meal.

When Charlie was gone, the old warden was quick to remark, "Now that's my cut of a man."

TWENTY-SIX
The Ice Fishery

Goddards Caddis

Across the frozen lake, in a sheltered inlet, a distant campfire twinkles in the lee of shoreline evergreens. Its curling grey smoke drifts high above the lake's surface, forming a haze against the forested hillside. The scent of frying trout drifts from the open campfire and across the lake. Seated by the fireside is a warmly clad ice-fisherman. He busies himself with the detailed preparations of a winter cookout. Strewn around him on the ice are lunch packs, fishing creels, tackle boxes, snowshoes and snowmobiles. Voices can be heard from inside a nearby fishing hut.

In the hut, more anglers sit in a circle around a fishing hole. They drop baited hooks to different depths of the compound and wait for a tug from below. Phantoms below the ice, huge trout and other game fish mill about waters untested by hook and line. Then a strike is experienced! A fishing tale or a shanty song is interrupted as a flouncing fish is hauled onto the ice surface. For these outdoors lovers, this is the best kind of fun.

Such is the scene on many of New Brunswick's lakes throughout the annual ice fishing period.

Since it was established during the late 1970s, many outdoor buffs have found relief from cabin fever in seeking distant lakes and fishing their waters. Speckled trout, yellow perch and pickerel provide excellent angling on more than 70 lakes throughout the province. All can be reached with little effort. Modern travel by cross-country skis or the family snowmobile has made even remote areas more accessible. It is said that many of these lakes can be reached more easily in winter than in spring. These rarely fished waters can thus supply fishermen with record-size fish in good numbers.

Many lakes are now stocked. Pan-size, hatchery-raised speckled trout are trucked in huge tanks from the Minto ponds and deposited in the more accessible lakes throughout the province. To ensure ample food supplies, they are stocked at the rate of eight fish per 100 feet of shoreline by marine biologists from the Department of Natural Resources. Biologists claim that newly stocked trout require a few days in a new lake to adjust to water conditions and become acclimatized enough to feed.

Bowing to the lure of a stocked fishing hole, some of us set out one Saturday afternoon in February for Shaddick Lake, about 15 miles from Newcastle in Northumberland County, and two miles from the community of Wayerton on the Chapel Island highway. We had picked up our ten-dollar fishing licences at the ranger station in Newcastle and received instructions from ranger biologists Bob Currie and Bernie Dubee. Currie spearheaded the Northumberland ice fishery and can boast one of the most successful in the province. After an anxious station wagon ride through rolling woodlands, we arrived at a parking lot overlooking the lake.

Shaddick Lake had been stocked with 2,000 speckled trout during the early winter and there were many abandoned fishing holes marked with tall evergreens. We each fished three lines, about six feet apart, using kernel corn as bait. By late afternoon we had seven plump speckled trout in our creels.

The season opens on the first of January and goes until March 31st. Roadways and parking lots are sometimes kept open in winter to give way to lakes that have been stocked and those located nearer townships. In the case of some lakes such as Grand Lake, fishing shanties have been constructed to encourage families to take part in the winter sport fishery. Prefabricated shanties can be assembled in a jiffy and are permitted on any given lake. They must bear the name and address of the owner in letters and numbers at least two inches high. Many anglers have used portable kerosene heaters in fishing huts. All huts must be removed from the ice surface by April 15th.

Fishing methods have not changed. Holes are made through the ice with long shaft augers. Five holes can be fished per angler, and all fishing lines must be in sight. Five trout per day is a winter fisherman's bag limit and kernel corn, raw meat, strips of bacon and artificial angle worms are used for bait. The use of finned fish such as perch is not permitted as bait. Unattended ice fishing holes larger than ten inches in diameter must be marked with an evergreen tree or a pole exceeding six feet in length. Officials from the Department of Natural Resources have emphasized that ice fishermen should be careful not to litter at campsites or on lake surfaces. Many lakes are patrolled daily.

Angling licences can be obtained at any provincial Forest Services office. Charts and maps showing stocked lakes as well as waters containing wild trout, perch, pickerel, landlocked salmon and bass are also available.

TWENTY-SEVEN
Muddy Water

Kola Fly

Joe has more time on his hands than his tired old body can make use of, and he enjoys only the mornings when he is rested. By evening his bones are sore and aching. He can't see as far as he used to — unless, of course, he is looking back. He regrets not having followed his dreams; the fear, and the years wasted. And there is pain he can no longer remember, no longer feel, but knows only that he has had it, and virtue too.

But nothing is the way it was; no longer can he smell a violet, and a blueberry doesn't taste as sweet. No longer can he feel a woman's kiss or hear the distant honk of geese that once turned his eyes toward Heaven to glimpse the wavering V's heading north between the clouds. No longer, no longer.

He scolds his grandchildren for playing their loud music, muddying his memories — the best times, the sweeter the longer ago they were. He sits in silence, rocking on the veranda, the summer when he was 12 resurfacing . . .

He is poling his father's boat over the brown gravel shallows and through the deep and dark eddies, scummed now with pollen. There is water in the boat and it is warm and scalding his bare feet as he tries to keep a solid footing on its slippery bottom. Because he is wearing cut-off pants and no shirt, he has been stung several times by mosquitos and once by an irritating horsefly. Joey's long blonde hair falls over his eyes. It is a very hot day with not a breath of wind, not a leaf stirring. The river is smooth between the choppy shallow bars that chuckle as he passes. The old board boat skims the water and the pole grinds the rocky bottom, dripping cold water on his legs. Behind the boat, the small waves spread out, wrinkling the surface downstream to both shores. Once in a while a meadow hen or a crane is spooked from along the shore, splattering the rocks as it reluctantly labours away.

He glances down at the long waving strands of eel grass and the algae-covered rocks and the small chubs and trouts that dart away from the boat. Also on the bottom are the long, openmouthed lamprey; some dead and some dying as they twist and roll on the slime-covered rocks of the eddies or face into the currents of the gravel salmon beds. Above the water's edge, there are skeletons of shad clinging to bushes: their eye sockets swarming with flies, their backbones white thorny-tailed snakes. He can smell the shore roses but the stench of the shad is overpowering and they blend into pockets of sweet-sour odour.

He has poled to these ledges every day since summer started. Here, away from the scent of hay-fields and farm animals, the cool river smells dominate. He loses track of time and often stays out past supper so that his mother is cross with him.

Everything is green: trees, shore grass, even the water. He gets thirsty and scoops up handfuls and it is clear and cold and sweet-tasting. He sees himself as if in one of those clear plastic paperweights you shake so that the water inside animates a country scene of green grasses waving in the breeze; his own pleasure dome, a world he knows and trusts.

He is living for this day only and all days past, now less than whole as this day has become. He is sure of the past and knows only that the future brings unwanted change. There is no reason to believe otherwise. He blocks it out of his mind. For a moment he is the river that never stands still, never sleeps day or night, winter or summer, but keeps rushing . . . rushing to the sea like a lemming; like time that never sleeps; old time, slow time, time that runs with him and around him and through him and tries to control him. And always it is in a hurry, hurry.

"Why hurry little river, why hurry to the sea," he quotes the school poem. "There is nothing there to do but to sink into the blue and all forgotten be." He knows the river, like time, is ageless and he struggles now to stay within its green hills and gravel shoals, its silent eddies with their tight-rooted grassy bottoms.

Along the banks and farther up into the hemlock ridges, he hears the robins, jays, stacatto-sounding woodpeckers and yellow-hammers that shatter the silence. He can taste the damp smells of fish and water and distant hay-fields and it all reminds him of the pre-school days and playing in the brook that ran past the house with its water-bugs, polywogs and frogs. Sensing him a natural enemy, they always scamper away, riling the brook's sandy bottom. He poles and thinks of the ledges and the big salmon that lie in the deep water below them. He had seen them every day for over a week, barely visible against the amber bottom — seven large salmon and three smaller ones, grilse.

Today the ledges and river are still shaded by the hemlock ridge. Lying flat on the ledge, he uses his palms to shade his eyes. He counts the tails that stroke the water like soft, wide brushes. "Always look for tails," his father had told him, "and the white ridges of the breathing gills." Joey knows that when it rains and the water rises, they will move on to the uppermost reaches of the headwaters, challenging the rapids and the beaver dams. He watches them — each one a missile ready to rocket, each with the ability to unravel even the most composed angler into fits of story-telling and each with the delicate flavour that tops the menu at the most exclusive hotel dining rooms. He knows; his father told him so.

The cork of the bamboo rod is warm in his hands, the peacock fly is on the leader. His heart thumps as he holds his breath and makes a delicate cast and the fly swings over them. They move only slightly, spooked by the line. He sees his distorted reflection staring back at him. There is no breathing now, no vision above the water, no thought but tranquil fish thoughts, thinking: We are not interested. We are too busy doing nothing; content in our nescience. No one else knows we're here . . . but can you keep a secret?

He turns away from the water now, his yaw-shaped reflection pulling into the ledge. He looks toward the sky and smokes a flat cigarette as squirrels chatter on the ridge behind him. He blindly tosses his cigarette butt into the water where it twists and turns in the tiny whirlpools. A salmon comes to the surface, making a boil on top of the water, and picks it up.

He drifts into sleep and there are fish swimming in his brain, bigger than life . . . fish swimming everywhere. There are partridge in the trees and the squirrels scold as he chases them from limb to limb, tree to tree. There are always plenty of squirrels here. The ridge has a brown layer of needles sprinkled over the sponge-like moss; soft and quiet under his feet.

He has a good sling-shot, made from the red rubber of a bicycle tube, an even maple crotch and the pouch from the tongue of a discarded shoe. He has gathered rocks along the railway, round and square rocks. Good rocks are hard to find . . . must be round to go go straight. He also has a few clouded marbles which he keeps for the most important shots. His pockets are heavy and they chafe his legs and he longs for the day when he can have a real gun.

Then he hears the scream of a yellow-hammer, a human cry. The ridge's hemlock become a story-book, the old school reader. Each tree has a yellow ribbon, its treasure a pot of gold, and the woodpecker is a little old lady with a white apron and a red handkerchief in her hair. He hated those lessons, hated school. He looks at himself and he is too small and there is a big buckle on his coat. He is unsure of his place, his time; unsure in the sleeping mists that drifts away now.

He is awake on the ledge, uneasy knowing that he has stayed on the river too long again. He wants to get home so his father won't punish him for wasting his time. Father has work for him to do . . . help with the haying and the chores.

The fish are lighter in colour now and lying nearer the surface. Joey takes off the peacock fly and ties a double-pronged hook to the leader. He throws it well out over them and, when it drops to the bottom, pulls it very slowly and carefully until the hooks are near the big salmon's back. He gives the line a yank, sinking the hooks firmly into its scaly side.

Surprised by the sudden sting, the fish turns and scoots away from the pool, making the reel screech, stirring the gravel and frightening the other fish. Joey's first reaction is a rueful laugh. Then he braces himself, leaning against the fish's power, making the rod bow, until he is able to tow the fish backward around the perimeter of the ledge. The fish jerks and jostles, leaping out of the water in frustration. When, finally, it starts to lose its strength, Joey is able to back it up fast, cutting off its oxygen as water rushes through its open gills. Finally he pulls the helpless fish, flapping, onto the rocks. He pounds it on the head with a heavy stone until its eyes begin to bulge. Joey has seen this look many times before on snared rabbits and other wildlife he has killed.

It is the look of death.

There is only a tiny flash of guilt, quickly overpowered as he realizes how proud his father will be when he comes home with the big salmon. He tosses the murdered fish into the boat, washes his hands and lights another cigarette to celebrate his catch.

He gets into the boat and starts to drift. The day is very hot and there are cobwebs in his brain. Diving over the edge, he swims all the way around and then climbs back into the boat to dry off in the sun. He catches a horsefly and it buzzes, tickling his palm, so he crushes it and tosses it on the water for a chub to rise for.

The river turns from green to blue as an uneasy wind comes up, turning the leaves so he can see their pale, webbed bottoms. He lies in the boat's dry end, drifting on a natural course, his feet over the side . . .

Joe hears the distant screams of children — further off, then near. He can hear the music machines and he struggles now to stay in the dream, stay in the boat. But he is in a different river now, a different boat.

The boy's river has become the man's; one of stagnant water with silt plugging up the spawning beds. The ridges along its banks are barren of trees, the earth brown and baked. He covers himself from the sun, continuing to drift more slowly now toward an ocean where there are no fish, and as he drifts, there are no birds to break the silence.

About the Author

W ayne Curtis was born near Blackville, New Brunswick, and studied at St. Thomas University. He is
author of the non-fiction collection *Currents in
the Stream* and the novel *One Indian Summer*. His
fiction has been published in literary magazines such as *The
Pottersfield Portfolio, The Cormorant* and *New Maritimes*
and has been dramatized on CBC Radio. In 1993 he won the

David Adams Richards
Award for short fiction.
Wayne Curtis currently
lives in Newcastle, New
Brunswick, where he is
a freelance journalist and
New Brunswick field
editor for *Eastern Woods
and Waters. Fishing the
Miramichi* is his third
book.